Twayne's United States Authors Series

EDITOR OF THIS VOLUME

David J. Nordloh

Indiana University

Adelaide Crapsey

TUSAS 337

ADELAIDE CRAPSEY

By EDWARD BUTSCHER

TWAYNE PUBLISHERS
A DIVISION OF G. K. HALL & CO., BOSTON

Library of Congress Cataloging in Publication Data

Butscher, Edward.
Adelaide Crapsey.

(Twayne's United States authors series ; TUSAS 337)
Bibliography: p. 120-25
Includes index.
1. Crapsey, Adelaide, 1878-1914. 2. Authors,
American—20th century—Biography. I. Nordloh,
David.
PS3505.R277Z6 1979   811'.5'.2 [B]   78-26595
ISBN 0-8057-7273-1

In Memory Of My Mother
LENA BUTSCHER (née CUTILLO)
1906-1976

Contents

About the Author

Edward Butscher has taught at the New School for Social Research and the C. W. Post Poetry Center. His poetry, reviews, critical essays, and short stories have appeared in a wide variety of magazines, including the *Georgia Review, The Nation,* the *Carleton Miscellany, Poetry Northwest, Poetry* (Chicago), and *Twentieth Century Literature.* He is the author of *Sylvia Plath: Method and Madness* and two collections of his own poetry, *Poems About Silence* and *Amagansett Cycle.* His poetry has also appeared in several anthologies, including *New American Poetry* and *Group '74,* which he co-edited for the N. Y. Poets' Cooperative, and he has recently edited and introduced *Sylvia Plath: The Woman and the Work* for Dodd, Mead. He is presently working on a critical biography of Conrad Aiken.

Preface

Adelaide Crapsey remains a bit of an enigma to the reading public, even to that very special public devoted to reading American poetry. Although her verses, which first appeared several months after her tragic death at the age of thirty-six in 1914, were greeted with much acclaim and eventually earned the respect of critics as diverse as Yvor Winters on the one hand and Horace Gregory and Marya Zaturenska on the other—the latter husband-and-wife team praised Crapsey in *A History of American Poetry* for being "as fine a minor talent as has ever appeared in American poetry"—they have never resulted in their author's attracting the serious attention she obviously deserves. Indeed, except for a handful of cinquains which have become a staple for certain anthologies, her poetry remains virtually unknown, and her life has been similarly slighted. The last (and sole) biography was written in 1933.

The main impetus behind this book, then, is to resurrect the reputation of a poet who was a pioneer in developing and perfecting a form of short lyric that was both highly personal and highly compressed in expression, as well as prophetically modern in its accent upon the despair of a mind unable to accept the religious certainties inherited from an earlier age. It also attempts to define the precise nature of Crapsey's achievement, where it began, how it evolved, what influences helped shape it. And the crucial relationship between life and art cannot be neglected in the process, if only because Crapsey was one of the first American poets, male or female, to venture into the dangerous shoals of personal confession—not that she was a confessionalist by any means, but that she placed fewer barriers between her immediate situation and her persona's perceptions of that situation than did her contemporaries.

Chapter One is a broad survey of Crapsey's life and art, an effort to view the biography within the context of the poetry and the larger literary world that nourished it. It also provides a brief, but essential, discussion of available texts. Chapter Two offers an analysis of the poems, criticism, and short stories which Crapsey wrote and published at Vassar while a student there, as a means of illuminating the poet's aesthetic in its infancy. Chapter Three concentrates upon *A Study in English Metrics*, the incomplete critical work that had occupied so much of Crapsey's spare time from 1902 onward; this treatise is interesting in its own right for the insights it supplies into the technical accomplishments of important poets like Milton and Thompson, but of even greater value as a way of ascertaining the personal approach to prosody of its author. Chapter Four treats the poems before 1911 in terms of major influences, assaying a rough chronological treatment from internal evidence for the most part, and isolates their particular strengths and weaknesses, especially as these are relevant to the subsequent emergence of the cinquains and other mature poems. Chapter Five is devoted exclusively to the invention of the cinquain and to a close critical examination of almost all the cinquains Crapsey ever composed, tracing the sources of the form and identifying those aspects of the cinquain which made it unique. Other late poems—at least those which could be positively described as such or seem to be so on the basis of technical and/or thematic evidence—are discussed in Chapter Six, although no attempt has been made to deal with Crapsey's "Cherokee Indian Charms," a brief, well-intentioned try at transforming prose translations into poetry that has no intrinsic literary value. Chapter Seven summarized Crapsey's general achievement and attempts to place her work into proper historical focus.

EDWARD BUTSCHER

Acknowledgments

Special thanks must go to the entire staff of the Department of Rare Books, Manuscripts, and Archives at the University of Rochester Library, and in particular to Mary M. Huth, Assistant Librarian, and Alma B. Creek, Manuscripts Assistant, for their aid with the Crapsey Papers. Other librarians were equally generous with their time and skills, including Frances Goudy, Special Collections Librarian, Vassar College; Mary B. Trott, Assistant Archivist, The Archives, Smith College; and Carmela Kinslow of the University of Notre Dame Memorial Library. Sister Mary Ambrose, St. Mary's Convent, Milwaukee, Wisconsin, also supplied valuable information, and Professor Susan Sutton Smith kindly saw to it that I received a copy of her dissertation on the poems and advance proofs of her edition of the poems and letters.

The quotations from *Verse*, by Adelaide Crapsey (Copyright 1922 by Algernon S. Crapsey and renewed 1950 by The Adelaide Crapsey Foundation) and *A Study in English Metrics*, by Adelaide Crapsey (Copyright 1918 by Esther Lowenthal) are reprinted by permission of Alfred A. Knopf, Inc. The material from *The Complete Poems and Collected Letters of Adelaide Crapsey* by Susan Sutton Smith is reprinted by permission of the State University of New York Press © 1976. The photograph of Adelaide Crapsey was supplied by and is used with the permission of the University of Rochester Library.

Gratitude of a more personal nature is gladly extended to Paula and Amy Rothholz for their continued support, and to Pudding and Miss Boo as well. A sadder, memorial vote of thanks goes to Godfrey, a good friend for seven years.

Chronology

1878   Adelaide Crapsey born September 9 in Brooklyn Heights,
       New York, the third child and second daughter of Rev.
       Algernon Sidney and Adelaide (Trowbridge) Crapsey.
1879   Crapsey family moved to Rochester, New York, where the
       Rev. Crapsey became rector of St. Andrew's Episcopal
       Church.
1884– Attended public schools in Rochester.
1893
1893– Sent to Kemper Hall, an Episcopal boarding school in
1897   Kenosha, Wisconsin, with sister Emily (born 1877). Studied
       Latin and French and edited the school magazine. Graduated
       as class valedictorian.
1897– Entered Vassar College, where she managed a basketball
1901   team, appeared in several plays, belonged to the debating
       team, was class poet for last three years, and served as
       editor-in-chief of the *Vassarion* (yearbook) in her senior year;
       graduated with honors and was elected to Phi Beta Kappa.
       Sister Ruth (age 11) died of undulant fever in 1898, and sister
       Emily (age 24) died of appendicitis in 1901.
1902– Returned to Kemper Hall to teach history and literature. First
1904   signs of serious fatigue appeared.
1904   Sailed for Europe in October to study at the School of
       Archaeology in Rome. Worked occasionally as lecturer and
       guide to earn extra money.
1905   Returned home late in the year to attend father's heresy trial
       in Batavia, New York.
1906   Rev. Crapsey formally deposed from Episcopal ministry.
1906– Taught literature and history at Miss Lowe's Preparatory
1907   School in Stamford, Connecticut. Older brother Philip (age
       31) died from the effects of malaria contacted years before
       during the Spanish-American War. Accompanied father to the
       Hague Peace Conference and on a walking tour of Wales in
       summer of 1907. Exhaustion became more of a problem; often
       had to spend weekends in bed.

1908   Family moved to new Rochester home in January. Forced to leave Miss Lowe's in December due to failing health.

1909– Returned to Europe for vacation and study, living first in
1911   Rome, then London and Kent. Spent months of February and March, 1909, in the Anglo-American Hospital in Rome. European sojourn characterized by exhaustion, continued poor health, severe financial problems, and intensive research in the London Museum for work on a study of English metrics.

1911   Returned to America in February and became instructor in poetics at Smith College. Invented the cinquain. Informed in summer that her disease was tuberculin meningitis, which was attacking the lining of her brain, but did not tell family.

1911– Continued to teach at Smith and work on metrical study.
1912

1913   Collapsed in July, 1913, while vacationing in Tyringham, Massachusetts, and taken to a hospital in Pittsfield. Sent from there to a private nursing home at Saranac Lake, New York. Began writing many of the cinquains and other poems that would subsequently appear in the various posthumous editions of *Verse*.

1914   Returned home to Rochester in August, where she died on October 8 of "chronic pulmonary tuberculosis."

CHAPTER 1

Life and Art

IN Yeats's magnificent, self-searching poem "The Circus Animals' Desertion," the poet asks, "Those masterful images because complete/Grow pure in mind, but out of what began?" Whether rhetorical or sincere, the question leads back to self, the poet as artificer. Even if ultimately unconscious, the images of poetry have their strongest roots in the specific soil of the poet's life, the interior, nonabstract life where darkness encourages those metaphorical connections an outer biography might never countenance or even admit.

This is certainly true of Adelaide Crapsey, although the pathetic circumstances surrounding her relatively brief life tended to exaggerate the difference between public self and poetic persona, especially in the poetry which came after 1910. Crapsey's letters home to family and friends during the final three years of her life (1911-1914), first from Europe, then from the sanatorium at Saranac Lake in New York, etch in the portrait of a brave, cheerful, sophisticated, generally optimistic young woman intent upon exploring and enjoying a world constructed upon sensible Christian principles.[1]

The gay portrait contrasts sharply with the death-obsessed voice of harrowing rue that emerges from the poetry of that same late period. Cinquains such as "November Night," "Triad," "Trapped," "The Guarded Wound," "Night Winds," "Amaze," "The Warning," and other, more traditional verses—for example, "Song," "Angélique," "Mad-Song," "Night," "The Sun-Dial," "Chimes," "The Lonely Death," and "To the Dead in the Grave-Yard Under My Window"—betray the genuine fear and occasional bitterness of a mind that knows it is sinking into oblivion. The possibility of spiritual transcendence is never completely abandoned or denied, at least not for very long, but poem after poem projects a narrow, though intense, vision of human destiny where a kind of secular cynicism holds sway. Indeed, the power of these verses, which include the finest

15

Crapsey ever wrote, resides precisely in their courageous refusal to soften crag edges of despair with vague appeals to the immortality of the soul or similar Romantic sentiments. It is this power which makes them modern, prophetic, and which emphasizes the extent to which Crapsey's poetic voice, like Emily Dickinson's several decades earlier, was unique to its time and place (America)—foreshadowing the shift toward the lyrical candor of an Edna St. Vincent Millay.[2]

And yet a potent, steady alternate current, which flowed equally strongly in the vivacious young woman limned by the letters, also spoke in her: the measured, humorous, sometimes pedantic dips and eddies of an intellect schooled in traditional literature and culture, restrained by middle-class proprieties. Even while carving out her bleak winter landscapes of private outrage and godless desolation, Crapsey was also busily composing much more conventional poetry on the order of "Grain Field," "Doom," "Perfume of Youth," and "The Mourner," in which death plays a secondary role to inherited, trusted religious and Romantic concepts. Though still death obsessed thematically, the voice here is wedded to the rigid lyrical dialectic of previous eras, a dialectic which can conceive of material phenomena as mere fluff before the solid convictions of a neoPlatonic faith in metaphysical ideals.

In general terms, the development of Crapsey's poetic skills follows a clear pattern of rising achievement, one easily charted as corresponding to the increasing pressures, mental and physical, of a terminal illness. Put simply, the sicker she grew, the nearer to death, the more effective and original Crapsey became as a poet. In many ways, her remarkable career echoes the fatal progress of Sara Teasdale's later journey toward authentic poetic consciousness, even though Teasdale's life had a more normal span and suicide for its climax.[3]

I   Family Background

Because her life and art were so visibly, so essentially intertwined, Adelaide Crapsey's biography assumes fundamental significance in understanding her poetry. And that biography has been the subject of only one study from the time of her death in 1914 until now, which further indicates the lack of importance attached to her achievement by subsequent generations.[4]

Adelaide Crapsey was born on September 9, 1878, in Brooklyn Heights, New York, the daughter of Rev. Algernon Sidney Crapsey, a well-read, free-thinking Episcopal minister, and his wife Adelaide (née Trowbridge), a reserved, intelligent, and energetic woman who tended to treat her brood of eleven children with distant affection. Ever the idealist, Rev. Crapsey abandoned his post as junior assistant minister in the affluent Trinity parish soon after his daughter's birth because, he felt, money and class played too large a role in church affairs.[5] He chose, instead, to accept the rectorship of St. Andrew's Episcopal Church in Rochester, New York, which meant the sacrifice of a secure four thousand dollars a year in salary for the uncertain sum of about fifteen hundred dollars a year deducted from "the pennies of the collection" at St. Andrew's each Sunday. But neither the move to Rochester nor reduced financial circumstances seemed to have unduly affected the family's relatively comfortable middle-class life style—or hindered the arrival of eight more siblings.

The home life of the Crapsey clan appears to have been both traditional and radically exciting, both refined and casual. Surrounded by hordes of books—philosophy, religion, classical authors—in a minister's tidy, if active, household, where the Bible was a constant source of information and poetry, Adelaide Crapsey began writing verses at an early age, though it was her maternal grandmother, not her mother, to whom she showed them. In fact, Mary Osborn, Crapsey's biographer, has noted: "Not until after the daughter who was named for her was dead did Mrs. Crapsey know that she had been a poet."[6] The mother apparently was too busy with household chores and taking care of new arrivals to notice much of anything, perhaps temperamentally unsuited to the role of confidante as well.

The most significant family relationship for the nascent poet, besides her close ties to Emily, her elder sister by a year, was with her father. Their union was emotional and intellectual, encompassing spirited exchanges at the dinner table and countless parlor discussions on highly mature topics, such as biblical interpretations, current political events, and deeper philosophical questions.[7] When charged with heresy by his church in 1905 for his refusal to accept the New Testament as a literal document, Rev. Crapsey took along his daughter Adelaide, not his wife, to the heresy trial. She would also accompany him to the Hague Peace Conference in the summer of 1907, and is the only one of his eleven children mentioned by name in his autobiography, *The Last of the Heretics*.[8]

As his autobiography affirms, Rev. Crapsey was a highly individualistic thinker who loved literature and could proclaim with pride near the end of his life that in "successive stages of my career I have been influenced by the master minds of Newman, Darwin and Karl Marx."[9] He was also a genuine Christian in his conviction that the preachings of Christ demanded concrete social action, not ritualistic adherence to obsolete dogmas and myths. His position led him to become increasingly involved with poor relief, prison reform, oppressive working conditions, and similar controversial issues, not the least of which was his well-known belief that his own church and others had been corrupted by money and politics into becoming the exclusive domains of the very rich.

Rev. Crapsey had a busy pen—undoubtedly an influence on his daughter—and never hesitated to publish his liberal, sometimes "radical" views on the crucial debates of the day in a steady stream of books and pamphlets.[10] In particular, he did not shy away from the publicity stirred up by his urbane notion that Jesus Christ had been a profound thinker and reformer rather than the mythical son of God capable of miracles, a notion which left him open to counterattacks from the conservative elements in the Episcopal Church who had been upset by his exposure of their failings.[11]

As a result of her father's literate and liberal ways, Adelaide Crapsey's intense Christian perception of reality, which never faltered for long on the personal level in the difficult years ahead, was always tinged with a humorous but compassionate awareness of human foibles, plus an enormous respect for intellectual accomplishments and the printed word. More important, Rev. Crapsey's patent affection probably helped mitigate the inevitable feelings of emotional neglect created by the presence of so many siblings and the benign remoteness of a somewhat preoccupied mother—besides trying to raise eleven children under reduced circumstances, Mrs. Crapsey also produced children's clothing at home for sale to supplement her idealistic husband's meager income, a project which led, in 1906, to the founding of "The Guild of the Lily," her own small firm.

By the time she and her sister Emily were sent to Kemper Hall—a parochial boarding school in Kenosha, Wisconsin, operated by Episcopal nuns—in the fall of 1893, Crapsey was already a mature, articulate, and generally pleasant young lady who related easily to her peers and seemed to possess the self-confidence of an adult. The only dark note had been sounded the year before, when she had been forced to miss an extended period of schooling due to a severe illness, the first she had suffered; but she had borne her discomfort with familiar, precocious fortitude, causing even her mother to write with warmth in her diary about her daughter's "wonderfully patient and sweet" attitude.[12]

II *Scholastic Settings*

From 1893 to 1913, a year before her death, Adelaide Crapsey's life would be dominated and defined by schools of one kind or another, first as student and then as teacher. On the positive side, this association did provide her with the means of and continuous access to a significant body of English and American literary knowledge, with the basic tools of her writing trade, and with a sympathetic environment that was conducive to its pursuit. But negatively it also encouraged a somewhat reclusive concept of aesthetic commitment, as an historical rather than an experiential function, and quite effectively cut Crapsey off from extended contact with the greater number of her fellow Americans in their various degrees of social and vocational interaction, and from most men—all the schools she attended or taught at were exclusively for women. Consequently, very often the rate and depth of her literary development, dependent as that was on useful experience, did not match the spectacular successes of her scholastic progress.

The four years Crapsey spent at Kemper Hall were marked by an unbroken series of academic and extra-curricular honors.[13] She played on the basketball team, appeared in several plays, and, along with Emily, was constantly involved with the *Kemper Hall Kodak*—a combination magazine and newspaper—from the very beginning of her high school career. She was an assistant editor for the 1895-96 semesters, then editor-in-chief the next year, which was the same course followed by her sister from 1894 to 1896.

Crapsey contributed regularly to the *Kodak* during her tenure at Kemper Hall, with items that ranged from a positive review of Charles Reade's novel *Peg Woffington* through an article defending Charlotte M. Yonge, British novelist and supporter of the reforms in the Anglican Church initiated by Newman and other members of the "Oxford Movement," to a number of slight stories that almost always dealt with sophisticated young men identified only by their last names.[14] She also published a translation of Alphonse Daudet's "The Pope Is Dead," a testament to her amazing ability to master foreign languages, which included finishing four years of Latin study in only two and winning the school's French prize in 1896. In this same year

Emily was chosen valedictorian, and her father came to deliver the commencement address.

Crapsey was also valedictorian when she graduated a year later, and delivered her address on Commencement Day, June 10, 1897.[15] Then she left for a summer vacation with the family at Lake Ontario, a vacation marred by the fatal illness of her younger sister Ruth. In September she went on to Vassar College, where she acquitted herself with equal success as an English major apparently determined upon a teaching career—one of the few fields open to women at the time. The courses she took and the literature she published in the school magazine are discussed fully in chapter two, and it is only necessary to note here that she achieved enough poetic fame at Vassar to be named class poet for her last three years there and became a close friend of Jean Webster, popular author and grandniece of Mark Twain, probably serving as a model for many of Webster's *Patty* sketches.

After leaving college in 1901—she had been elected to Phi Beta Kappa and graduated with honors—Crapsey spent a year at home before returning to the friendly confines of Kemper Hall, where she taught history and literature for the next two years. During this time she began to experience the symptomatic fatigue that would, with ever increasing regularity, burden the rest of her short life.

It was while teaching at Kemper Hall that Crapsey decided to devote much of her time to a study of English prosody, affected particularly by the metrical brilliance of Milton, whose work she had always deeply admired. Writing her own poetry remained a casual affair.[16] She apparently envisoned herself as à scholar, not a poet, and eventually destroyed many of the poems written before 1911. But, at several levels, poetry would be regarded as a technical matter to the very end—a reflection, perhaps, of the surface control Crapsey had to maintain as tuberculosis bored relentlessly into her brain. Such restraint was to be the weakness and strength of her best verses.

Between 1904 and 1906, Crapsey studied at the School of Archaeology in Rome, accompanied her father to his heresy trial in Batavia, New York, and had to deal with the death of her elder brother Philip from the effects of the malaria he had contacted during his service in the Spanish-American War. In 1906 she accepted an appointment as instructor in literature and history at Miss Lowe's Preparatory School in Stamford, Connecticut, where she would remain for two years. The tenure at Miss Lowe's was characterized by more frequent bouts of fatigue, which often resulted in weekends spent in bed, although Crapsey did accompany her father to the

Hague Peace Conference and on a walking tour of Wales in the summer of 1907.

Failing health caused Crapsey to resign from Miss Lowe's in December, 1908, but she soon sailed for Europe—she had not informed her family about her fatigue problems—and lived there in near poverty until February, 1911.[17] In terms of aesthetics, this European experience proved crucial to her poetic awakening. Her continued pursuit of a study into English metrics, her tedious labor over the "application of phonetics to metrical problems,"[18] undoubtedly spurred her subsequent interest in Japanese poetry, which, in turn, would lead into the creation of the cinquain form. Professor Susan Sutton Smith's thorough study of Crapsey's reader slips from the British Museum between April, 1910, and February, 1911, has indicated "a widely varied and yet intensive program of reading in poetry, metrics, phonetics, and aesthetics."[19]

Immediately upon returning to America early in 1911, Crapsey became an instructor in poetics at Smith College. She taught two courses, "The Principles of Exposition" and "Poetics: A Critical Study of Verse Forms," and spent most of her spare time, when not bedridden by fatigue, in the airless English Seminar Room at the Smith College Library, either counting syllables for her prosody study or making copies of her own poems.[20] It was at Smith that she began dressing completely in grey, a final variation upon her earlier habit of wearing only brown or beige outfits, which, if nothing else, saved her from the need of being in fashion.[21] Here, also, Crapsey made the acquaintance of Esther Lowenthal and Mary Delia Lewis, colleagues and sympathetic supporters of her work.

During the summer of 1911, Crapsey was finally diagnosed as having tuberculin meningitis, which she must have suspected with dread all along. She did not inform her family of the diagnosis, however, and returned in the fall to Smith, to teach, to count syllables, and to write her poetry. It was a year later, during a summer vacation in the Berkshires, that she collapsed and had to be taken to a hospital in Pittsfield, Massachusetts. With only a brief visit home in between, she was sent from there to Trudeau's, a private nursing home at Saranac Lake, New York, where she would remain from September, 1913, until August, 1914.

This year, which involved many painful treatments and forced airings in below-freezing temperatures, witnessed an amazing burst of creativity, comparable, in a minor way, to Keat's own last surge. As the doctors inflicted their various, futile techniques upon her weakened body, Crapsey wrote most of the cinquains which would make *Verse* the unique collection it is. Battered from optimism to despair and back again with almost daily regularity, she felt death slowly crushing the breath out of her, and struggled to poetically encompass and preserve the emotional onslaught she was experiencing.

On a personal level, what is truly remarkable about this plague year was the cheerful courage Crapsey displayed as she fought back against a disease she must have now known was fatal. The letters she wrote (sometimes with great physical effort) from the sanatorium provide a moving glimpse into the sheer strength of character that kept her mind and imagination functioning so fully during a period of growing despair—above all, the cinquains are models of cool craftsmanship. The despair itself is almost never alluded to by Crapsey, who constantly played down the seriousness of her condition, and rarely do the letters touch upon the tedium and horror which were her day-to-day fare. Only once, in a letter to Esther Lowenthal dated September 25, 1913, does she concede that the "days, truth to tell, are rather long."[22] A month later, when her right side was paralyzed to the point where her script had become a scrawl, she dismisses the new symptom as "nothing serious."[23]

The doctors continued their inadequate treatments, causing Crapsey's hopes to rise and fall with each positive sign, however feeble. Late in November, she writes of a Dr. Edward R. Baldwin as being "openly optimistic," although earlier in the same month she had alluded to the "fresh and inexplicable weights of fatigue" that had settled down on her until "my pen lags and drags."[24] Crapsey liked and trusted Dr. Baldwin, appreciating his youth, humor, and compassion, and he wrote a memoir about their association. When he took over her case, he found her already under the terrible pressure of "advanced invalidism" and was struck, like so many of her contemporaries, by her intense need for privacy—her "shrinking and sensitive" spirit was "unsuited for association with other patients"— and by her rebelliousness when forced to surrender her study of metrics.[25]

Meanwhile, Crapsey tried to keep up with her reading as well as her writing, perusing the New York *Times* every day and the *Nation* every week, along with monthly cultural journals such as *Poetry* (Chicago) and the *Atlantic Monthly*, and a number of books, including a life of Francis Thompson, a critical collection by Henry James, a selection of poems by William Butler Yeats, and her own "little chunky brown bible," which she described as "Simon pure King James."[26] She also looked forward with excitement to reading the first issue of *Blast,* the radical Vorticist magazine promised from England.[27]

But literature and the pretenses of a normal, productive life could not forestall the internal death march. In desperation, the doctors attempted the "pneumothorax treatment," which involved collapsing one of Crapsey's lungs. Three times they tried without success,[28] the only concrete result being the poet's witty and pathetic "Lines Addressed to My Left Lung Inconveniently Enamoured of Plant-Life." Although she wrote about a time for "complete recovery" in the future, the early months of 1914 witnessed a steady decline in her health. The weariness increased, as did the monotony of her often bedridden existence—"if boredom killed I'd be many times a corpse."[29] And in April she experienced what she called "my latest calamity" and "what I dreaded beyond everything": without telling her first, her father had agreed with the Smith College authorities that his daughter should give up her teaching position for the next year.[30] In dismay, Crapsey had to thus abandon another dear illusion, contemplate "another year without work"—had to accept, in other words, the blunt fact of her deteriorating condition.

A letter from Crapsey to Esther Lowenthal of April 21 mentions a cough that "simply will not stop," and concedes the possibility of chronic tuberculosis, but still refuses to consider death as a logical, imminent terminus: "I'm just going to go ahead, find a way of living that's as little invalidish as possible, get what I can out of things and let it go at that."[31] By May 6, however, her depression aided by snowy, then rainy weather, she admits that she is "rather done and down— cough devilish for the last 3 or 4 weeks, now a head cold and a temperature to get rid of."[32] It had already been decided that Crapsey's life would end in a sanatorium, and a search was on for one closer to home and in a less frigid climate. Her letter of May 16 bitterly notes that "It's a gay life" before reasserting the happy outer face, concluding with a light-hearted denial of relentless decay: "All this written in bed—can't imagine why I've had this horrid slump."[33]

Self-mockery, cheerful indifference, almost childish innocence, these were Crapsey's last defenses, and she clung to them with stubborn valor. On May 19, alluding to the quest for a new sanatorium, she comments, "There is still, I may add, no tomb in sight," but also remarks with wistful rue that "It seems a million billion years since I was alive and on the job—(or half alive any how)."[34] In August she returned home to Rochester, too ill to read or write much, excited by the prospect of some of her poems appearing in the *Century Magazine*—Jean Webster had brought the special delivery letter of acceptance to her at Trudeau's. Further satisfaction came from the knowledge that, despite her illness, she had managed to organize a volume of the poems she wished preserved for publication.

On October 8, as polite and cheerful as ever, she passed away without ever seeing her poems in print. The book, however, would live for her: in Harriet Monroe's somewhat florid phrases, "the shadowed fire of her spirit burns on with singular intensity."[35]

III   *Literary Influences and Enthusiasms*

The literary influences on Adelaide Crapsey's life and art are not too difficult to trace and isolate, although her unique distinction as inventor and master of the cinquain anticipated rather than borrowed from the Imagist movement, Hulme's "forgotten school of 1908" in England. Yvor Winters has suggested—and his thesis is partly reinforced by any serious reading of her early work—that Crapsey was a child of her times poetically speaking, that she "had been heavily influenced by the poetry of the 'nineties', but learned skill, not mannerism."[36] Certainly, for a long while, Crapsey remained true to the styles and modes of her contemporaries, who would include, in America, Sidney Lanier, William Vaughn Moody, and other voices from what George Santayana later labelled "the Genteel Tradition."[37]

But it is not clear that Crapsey was directly influenced by the work of these or other American writers. Edward Arlington Robinson's *The Children of the Night* had appeared in 1897, for example, but there is no evidence that she had read or responded to it in any way, or that she assimilated Robinson's radical concept of poetic realism—a concept subsequently mined with effective drama by Edgar Lee Masters's *Spoon River Anthology* (1915). Nor was she likely to have welcomed the Whitmanesque crudities unleashed by Masters's partners in the "populist" revolt, Vachel Lindsay and Carl Sandburg, whose voices emerged between 1913 and 1916 to challenge the Imagist phenomena.

In fact, except for certain European influences, Crapsey's poetic career was shaped around an Emily Dickinson-like isolation from modern trends, despite her interest in contemporary magazines and her trips abroad. The past, not the present, held her attention. Her literary interests were primarily scholastic in aim and were concentrated in her many years of reading classic English authors for her planned work in metrics. As a result, "contemporary" authors for her meant figures from the late nineteenth century, such as Francis Thompson, Robert Bridges (whose metrical work on Milton absorbed her), Oscar Wilde, Lionel Johnson, and other Georgian poets, although the most beloved of British poets were undoubtedly John Keats and Walter Savage Landor, to whose lives and poetry she felt particularly close, identifying with the Romantic ethos they seem to have embodied.[38]

Her isolation, however, was never deliberate or parochial. Though perhaps not familiar with Arthur Symons's *The Symbolist Movement in Literature* (1899), which had such a crucial impact on T. S. Eliot and those members of his generation who found in the French Symbolists a new impulse towards inner intensity, Crapsey was fluent in French and, while in London, had read Baudelaire's work, albeit in translation.[39] She had also perused Beardsley's prose writings and was fully familiar with much of the *fin de siècle* movement in England and France, even if very little of its risqué lushness seeped into her own verses.

Her mastery of French, in fact, would eventually lead to the cinquain, since it was her reading of Michel Revon's 1910 translations in his *Anthologie de la Littérature Japonaise des Origines au XXe siècle* that apparently acquainted her with the haiku and tonka forms—which, in turn, inspired a desire for a similar English mode.[40] Her fascination with Japanese poetry preceded Ezra Pound's subsequent move in that direction by several years; Pound did not begin working from the manuscripts of Ernest Fenollosa, the Oriental expert who died in 1908, until the winter of 1913-14. Besides Revon, Crapsey read Yone Noguchi's *From the Eastern Sea*, a book of original verses and translations from the Japanese, and William N. Porter's English translations, *A Hundred Verses from Old Japan*.[41] She copied poems from both the Revon and Noguchi collections, a practice she followed only with poets whom she greatly admired.[42]

Rather than being an element in a conscious literary direction, then, Crapsey's pioneer work in the short form and her seeming link to the Imagists were actually the result of independent investigations, strengthened by a personal sense that restraint of a neoClassic kind was best suited to her consistent concern with technique. Imagism, after all, was simply another idea whose time had come, and Crapsey was not alone in her realization that the extravagant excesses of the Georgian and Genteel schools—from which her own verses were never completely free before her confinement in a sanatorium—had to find a purging counter-corrective, strangling "the neck of rhetoric" as Verlaine demanded. Amy Lowell, H. D., Ezra Pound, and their like were strangers to her, but she shared their conviction that emotion had to locate and be controlled by a highly compressed image—an emblem and/or symbol—that would suggest rather than insist upon deeper causal relationships.

In the same way, the "plain speech" that would appear in the finest of her cinquains was not indebted to the vernacular revolution launched by Robinson and Masters at home, but was the natural, practically inevitable consequence of the same drive toward a purer, less archaic form. This inclination in language was further stimulated by a life-long knowledge of and dependence upon the Bible, a constant companion, and reflected Crapsey's ingrained commitment to theological speculations. In her mind, religion and poetry, at least before her last year, were dual aspects of a human search for metaphysical realities. The parables and allegories which she took from the Bible and transferred into her poetry must have played their role in her growing appreciation of the power that lay in a shift away from the clutter of detail toward a sort of literary shorthand.

Finally, it is necessary to mention Crapsey's probable and significant debt to the poetry of Emily Dickinson. Dickinson, of course, who had died without having any sort of appreciable impact on her own generation, did not become an important figure in American poetry until the 1890s. Her reputation was affirmed in 1900 when Edmund Clarence Stedman's influential *An American Anthology* included a generous portion of her poetry.[43] Many poets of the late 1800s and early 1900s, such as Stephen Crane, tended to regard Dickinson as a contemporary,[44] and Crapsey herself might have been one of them, though no evidence exists to prove it.

But the speculative details are not as significant as the obvious debt to Dickinson that runs through Crapsey's later work: the whimsical tone, at times in conjunction with deathly serious topics, the intellectual playfulness, the obsession with death, the persistent need for brevity and directness, and even a taste for odd punctuation. From a strictly psychological standpoint, Crapsey's decision to wear grey from head to toe, which began at Smith—she actually "sometimes brought to class a thin, fully-sharpened gray pencil"[45]—was certainly more than an imaginative attempt to defeat the lack of stylishness imposed by a severe budget, as Professor Smith has concluded.[46] That total, almost coy, somewhat egotistical greyness appears to have been another way for Crapsey to express her belief that, like Dickinson, her ascetic literary mission in life required an appropriate external gesture.

IV *The Texts*

Except for material published in school magazines, newspapers, and yearbooks, the sad central fact about Adelaide Crapsey's texts is that they are posthumous. Crapsey did receive word that several poems had been accepted for publication by *The Century,* but died a month before the magazine appeared.[47] She had been arranging a book of her poems some months earlier with the aid of Esther Lowenthal and Mary Delia Lewis, clearly intending to leave it behind as a sort of combined last testament and self-memorial, which indeed confirms her acute consciousness of death's rapid approach: "Wouldst thou find my ashes? Look / In the pages of my book; / And as these thy hand doth turn, / Know here is my funeral urn."

As a result, the 1915 first edition of Crapsey's *Verse,* which was printed by her Rochester acquaintance and neighbor, Claude Fayette Bragdon, is the most accurate in terms of its author's personal preference, although Miss Lowenthal and Miss Lewis had exerted a limited amount of editorial authority after their friend's death; they deleted four poems, "The Death of Holofernes," "Refuge in Darkness," "Narcissus," and "The Entombment," and added two others, "Old Love" and "My Birds That Fly No Longer."[48] Furthermore, Bragdon inserted "To the Dead in the Grave-Yard Under My Window" on his own volition.

When Alfred A. Knopf took over Crapsey's work and printed a new edition of *Verse* in 1922—with the cooperation of the poet's mother—it incorporated all sixty-three poems from Bragdon's volume but changed Crapsey's punctuation to conform with more acceptable usage, utilized an earlier version of "To the Dead in the Grave-Yard Under My Window," and added seven poems: "For Lucas Cranach's *Eve,*" "The Source," "Blue Hyacinths," "Autumn," "The Elgin Marbles," "The Crucifixion," and "The Fiddling Lad" (originally "The Fiddler"), the first three of these cinquains. After two reprintings of this edition, Knopf issued another enlarged volume of *Verse* in 1934, which included twenty more poems: "Safe," "Warning to the Mighty," "Sad of Heart," "Blossoming plum and cherry,"

"Endymion," "The Entombment," "The Event," "The Companions,"
"Thou art not friendly sleep," "What News, Comrades," "Aubade,"
"John-a-dreams—," "Fragment," "Narcissus," "To a Hermit
Thrush," "Fresher/ Than spring's new scents" (with variant), "Why
have/ I thought the dew" (identified as a translation from French out
of the Japanese), "To an Unfaithful Lover," "The Death of
Holofernes," and "Languor After Pain"—the last six are cinquains.

But all of these editions have since been superseded by the
thorough, scholarly efforts of Professor Susan Sutton Smith, who
provided "The Poems of Adelaide Crapsey: A Critical Edition with
an Introduction and Notes" in 1971 as a doctoral dissertation,
working with Crapsey's own papers at the Rochester University
Library and calling upon the valuable aid of surviving friends and
relatives of the poet. In 1977, Professor Smith's *The Complete Poems
and Collected Letters of Adelaide Crapsey* was published by the State
University of New York Press in Albany, and it will surely remain the
definitive text of Crapsey's poetic canon, supplying, as it does, all
possible variants, extensive annotations, and the poet's own arrangement of her work, where available.[49]

For critical purposes, whether historically conceived or not, the
Bragdon edition was the one which created the most stir when it first
appeared and definied Crapsey's literary profile. It was this edition
which caused Llewellyn Jones to remark in his *New Republic* review
that *Verse* was "a book of poetry that will live,"[50] and led an
anonymous reviewer in the *Baltimore Post Express* to link Crapsey
with "this great company" of Heine, Baudelaire, and Poe in her
penchant for poems about "pain and death," the darker side of human
experience.[51]

From a more modern perspective, the 1915 edition of *Verse*. with
the restoration of the four poems deleted by Lowenthal and Lewis
and the excision of the two they had added, serves as an essential
fulcrum still, because it does offer the pattern projected by Crapsey
herself—like Bragdon, I think the inclusion of "To the Dead in the
Grave-Yard Under My Window" is basic, for thematic and stylistic
reasons. *Verse* makes clear that the cinquains and several other late
poems guarantee her a certain immortality as a significant minor poet
and as an American pioneer in the massive clearing away of dead
wood commenced by the Imagists in the early 1900s and later carried
forward through the major stream of the modernist movement
represented in the shorter lyrics of Ezra Pound and William Carlos
Williams.

Cinquains such as "The Warning," "Night Winds," "The Guarded Wound," "November Night," "Trapped," and "Triad," not only anticipate the Imagist revolt, while looking backward to the innovations initiated by Emily Dickinson, but also project a future sense of the universe in which religion has lost its power to protect man from awareness of his own mortality. The other late poems, particularly "To the Dead in the Grave-Yard Under My Window," offer the additional poetic value of a language that rejects artificial "stage speech" in favor of a voice closer to the vernacular, as well as a refreshing candor about personal feelings that could be described as less-than-heroic. More to the point, perhaps, *Verse* contains an impressive number of excellent poems that betray the virtue of all good poetry: lyric intensity, metaphoric originality, and a certain complexity of insight and structure.

CHAPTER 2

The Vassar Years (1897-1901)

ADELAIDE Crapsey's four years at Vassar were naturally years of apprenticeship as far as her literary development was concerned—full, busy, productive years, but years that saw little attempt to shape a new or unique voice. The past was being discovered, digested, and there was no Self to reveal, no secret "Soul" to captain and exploit, as if Walt Whitman had never existed. The poems and stories that survive from this period, especially the former, published and preserved in the *Vassar Miscellany* and the *Vassarion*, which Crapsey would edit in her senior year, evince an almost miraculous lack of interest in experimental styles and themes, although all of them demonstrate a precise, careful, restrained, rather heavy-handed awareness of literary history as well as a meticulous concern for craftsmanship.

As class poet at Vassar her last three years—a post she took very much to heart—Crapsey cast her own verses in traditional molds without question, and, not too surprisingly, they often read like pale imitations of the poets being discussed in the classroom. As an English major, she also immersed herself in a wide selection of courses that gave her a solid background in most areas of literary experience, varying from the standard, required "Composition" and "Argumentation" courses through the standard survey classes, such as "Development of English Literature from Beowulf to Swift," "Old English, Including Beowulf," and the inevitable "Shakespeare," to the more specialized, more contemporary "Nineteenth Century Poetry" and "Nineteenth Century Prose from Coleridge to Pater."[1] It is a very impressive list from any vantage point, but especially when considered as part of a program that also included courses on the "Development of Rhetorical Theory" and on the special problems of "Poetics," not to mention required "Psychology" and "Ethics" semesters, four years of German, a year each of mathematics, Latin, and chemistry, a two-year elective in history (European history), and three classes in economics.

30

What is striking by its absence is any course dealing specifically with the American experience and its literature. Though undoubtedly familiar with her nation's historical and cultural past, Crapsey had a college education which tended to slight the linguistic and technical revolution generated by *Leaves of Grass* and the parallel movement toward "realistic" psychological portraiture subsequently introduced by Edward Arlington Robinson (with a bow to Robert Browning, whose work Crapsey did know).[2] Thus the few American writers who do surface in her early work are usually the very ones least likely to offend public taste—a Poe with his archaic imprecisions of language and thought, or, in a more "modern" vein, a Sidney Lanier drifting off into his capitalized states of rhetorical ecstasy and stage sorrow.[3]

I *Undergraduate Poetry*

The poetry that appeared in the *Vassar Miscellany* between 1898 and 1901, usually competent enough to avoid total failure but far too glib for success at any level other than the ornamental, cleaves close to orthodox lyrical stances and concerns—romantic love, failure of romantic love, the price of personal isolation, time's slippery nature, and so on. And it uses traditional meters and rigid rhyme schemes that are frequently unable to carry the lead burden of their thematic truisms. Crapsey was listening too closely, too intently to Lanier and other equally traditional though more recent writers who refused to abandon the arch language of a misunderstood past, who still clung to the then fashionable ethos of art as a rarefied, if unredeeming, phenomenon where elitists dwelled. This could include Louise Imogen Guiney (1861-1920) and the young Sara Teasdale (1884-1933), along with a host of forgotten versifiers whose work filled the popular magazines of the day, such as *Scribner's,* the *Atlantic Monthly,* and *Harper's Weekly.* Harriet Monroe's more daring *Poetry* would not be founded until 1912.

And yet, sometimes with sly humor, a sense of perverse individuality does slither through the tangled net of echoes. In Crapsey's first published poem, "Loneliness" (137),[4] for instance—which seems to hearken back to Edgar Allan Poe's "Alone" for its inspiration—there is an uncharacteristic suggestion of godless despair and alienation.[5] Despite its weak imagery and string of unremarkable rhymes, the poem posits a genuine, child's-eye view of self and universe that plunges into complete nullity. It moves from grey mist, sea, and sky

to the grey dunes where the speaker stands in dismay, doubting her
culture's Christian heritage by depicting a God who has deserted her:

> Oh, if God there be, his face from me
>   The rolling gray mists hide;
> And if God there be, his voice from me
>   Is kept by the moan of the tide.

Part of this anguish is pure pose, of course, Wordsworth's "moan of
doves," a bright young girl expressing youth's ancient penchant for
shock techniques and melodramatic extremes, death and rebellion
seen as essential to a poet's bold signature. But the unrelieved aura of
blasphemous denial intimates the possibility of authentic alienation
and the existence of inner doubts. Though both tone and substance
remain in strict keeping with Poe's own mental set, reflecting a well
established vision of the artist trapped in creative (albeit desperate)
isolation, there is no saving frame of moral alternatives, no hint of
ironic distance. "Loneliness" is unique in the early Crapsey world; its
total despair will not surface again until the last months of the poet's
life. Therefore, the poem's technical failure seems less important
than its severe negativism—brought on, perhaps, by the death of
Crapsey's younger sister earlier in the year.
     Crapsey published another poem in the same issue of the *Miscel-
lany,* one called "Time Flies" (137), and the title alone should be
sufficient warning of what is to come: a solitary lover musing to
himself in the shadow of Marvell's garden, discovering that "Today
love's fled" and that "the hours swiftly by us go."[6] The language is
again pretentious, coyly sweet, and the imagery has no chariot to save
it from its blunt truisms: "Love and roses will never last." The
narrative voice, presumably female, begins by establishing the
clichéic conceit of a rose that bloomed briefly, gloriously with love,
but now has succumbed to relentless mortality: "Faded and fallen its
petals gay;/ The rose lies dead in the garden to-day." Much worse is
"e'n wist" and similar anachronisms, and the didactic determination
to find salvation beyond the temporal: "Then gaily speed past what is
over,/ And gladly greet new rose and lover."
     This greeting-card climax certainly fits the structure of the poem as
a whole, unsheathed from the English Renaissance of Campion and
aimed toward Shakespeare's "To love that well which thou must leave
ere long." Its jingling rhymes and meter, along with its insistent
alliterations, clang home with resounding heaviness. Crapsey was

only an impressionable college girl, after all, though a brilliant, well-read one, so the disappointment of her "imitations" should not cause much discomfort. And yet the utter absence of a poet's ear and eye, and the inability to conceive of (or at least communicate) complex states of consciousness and sensibility give no suggestion that the poet is storing enough powder for future explosions. Despite its display of learning, the talent here is minimal, which might suggest that either Crapsey was destined to be a natural late bloomer or, more likely, that she needed some powerful emotional tremor to wrench her imagination free from its tidy, timid, schoolgirl cage of fussy craftsmanship.

A month later, the *Miscellany* printed "The Heart of a Maid" (138), which offers no relief from her callow attempts to reproduce the English Renaissance without benefit of a more contemporary perspective.[7] The opening stanza immediately defines the poem's archaic limitations:

> Petals of the marguerite
> Tell me, pray,
> Doth he love me?—Answer
> "Yea" or "nay."

The sole note of originality enters through the response of the female narrator to the two contrary replies, casually dismissing her lover's possible love with "What care I?" but, when confronted by the opposite truth, weeping, "Let me die!" The "What care I?" is used as a refrain that then becomes ironic, a double-edged dagger, its tone sequentially assuming both indifference and despair. If nothing else, "Heart of a Maid" is clever—more clever than "Time Flies" certainly in its effort to introduce some sort of saving convolution—and retains a touch of charm.

Like the young Ezra Pound, the young Crapsey seemed most comfortable when translating rather than creating a poem, and in the next year she did just that with "Repentance" (138-9), which was adapted from the old French.[8] Unbothered by the need to invent situation and voice, she can manipulate the poem's physical reality without obvious strain, and her love of obsolete, neoClassical vocabularies does not appear as disconcerting as before, complementing, as it does, the aristocratic speaker's own era. If too pat, "Repentance" has the virtue of establishing a kind of playful urbanity which engages the reader and binds him to the poem's deliberate sham: "Aye, oft I've visited the court, / Made love to ladies—idle sport!" This is risqué in a pleasant, drawingroom fashion, and evinces a semblance of conversational ease. By poem's end, the anticipated climax also provides a smooth, almost parable-like justification for its cyclical slightness: "But now, alack! gay youth is spent; / I'm getting old—I'd best repent!" It is not difficult to imagine Crapsey's literate classmates smiling in admiration over the learned and mocking aptness of that closing couplet, appreciating how a fellow member of the Vassar "nunnery" might revel in the smallest hint of gay naughtiness—naughtiness filtered through the stained-glass rays of a schoolroom exercise in translation.

The last of Crapsey's poems to appear in the *Miscellany* came in a Christmas issue and is appropriately a prayer.[9] "Hail Mary!" (139)— the exclamation point is innocent of any irony—defies criticism; its entire purpose is to exist as Holy Script, to echo and to emphasize a plea directed at a heaven where received faith, not intelligence, rules supreme. Its lines cannot be assimilated today, when belief has retreated into psychology, although Crapsey herself probably de- sired deeply to perfect the unreal configuration of womanhood projected by her sincere poem—feminism was still only an economic issue at the time. "Loveliness," "purity," "faith," "grace," all the Madonna virtues are categorized, then celebrated by the inevitable petition for an equal perfection in the flesh:

> God give me grace to be like thee,
> That in my poor and low degree
> I, like thyself, may blessed be.
> Hail Mary!

That such a poem could see print in the *Miscellany* at the turn of the century speaks volumes about the sheltered, bookish world that nurtured and judged Crapsey, a world made even narrower by the further restraints imposed by a chaste women's college dedicated to inculcating the concept of the Fine Arts as a specifically female grace, duty, and social luxury. "Hail Mary!" confirms also that its author remained firmly moored to an aesthetic island far removed from the depths already being plumbed by Edward Arlington Robinson and by novelists like Stephen Crane and Henry James. It was an adolescent aesthetic, an aesthetic of escape, an innately conservative aesthetic that located its deepest anchor in European (English) currents.

II   *Undergraduate Prose*

In her work in prose, perhaps because not afflicted with any compulsion to reproduce "poetical" language, Crapsey was much more successful during her Vassar years. Her short stories and book reviews from the *Miscellany,* however precious on occasion, are easy reading. The four Crapsey stories that appeared in the *Miscellany*— "A Girl to Love," "The Knowledge He Gained," "Mr. Percival Poynton and a Pig," and "Milord and Milady"—share a certain light-hearted attitude toward character and experience that never wanders very far beyond the superficial plot twists common to an O. Henry tale. Though competent and expeditious, their narrative drive is always based upon a somewhat comic perception of an extremely limited social milieu, usually upper middle-class, and, as such, qualify as stories of manners, not morality; of caricature, not character.

The first of them, "A Girl to Love," concerns four young men, refined, college educated men, none of whom is more than an outline, representing four distinct responses to creativity and culture: Jimmy the artist, whose studio is the scene of the action; Faulkner, a journalist with a penchant for Aubrey Beardsley drawings; Reynolds, "a blase, cynical young lawyer of twenty-four, and Merriman, another artist, but "a purple-seeing impressionist."[10] The crux of the simple but sly plot revolves around the photograph of a beautiful young woman that the other three men discover in Jimmy's studio during his absence—he is in Paris for a few months—and are entranced by to the point of near obsession. Merriman paints her, Reynolds writes "heavy, philosophical love poems," and Faulkner develops an image of "an Ideal Woman, concerning whom he held forth at length."

The expected reversal to this brief narrative comes with Jimmy's return and the announcement that the photograph is actually of him, taken when he appeared in a female role for the Hasty Pudding play at Harvard. The naive artificiality of a story in which characters can exclaim "By Jove!" and "The deuce" reinforces the conventions associated with narratives of manners, and does not mar the economy of its presentation—anecdotal rather than developmental—or the straightforward unravelling of event. But neither does it permit any exploration of the subtle implications behind the central male-female confusion. What is important about "A Girl to Love" is the insight it supplies into Crapsey's keen awareness of contemporary mores, her

knowledge of modern painting—for example, of Impressionism and
Beardsley—and her ability (and desire) to poke fun at the class of
intellectuals which took such things seriously. It is essentially a
conservative thrust, though committed to art in a romantic context,
and yet one that also reflects a certain amount of real sophistication.

"The Knowledge He Gained," which is even briefer than "A Girl to
Love," is less successful in its contrivance, although art again plays a
crucial role.[11] In this case, the protagonist, a man simply identified as
Errington (heavy-handed Britishism), is a fiction writer working
alone on a beach, working on a short story. Having reached the climax
of his tale, he has found himself written into a corner: his heroine
must reveal a secret "told to her in strictest confidence" in order for
the plot to function properly, but he has already limned her "as a girl
who would keep her word under any circumstances." To resolve his
dilemma, he decides to have his heroine brush her hair with another
girl, knowing that girls cannot help divulging their most private
thoughts "while they are brushing their hair together."

With a loud offstage creaking of gears, fate intervenes through the
sudden arrival of two very wet young ladies in a rowboat, who are
coming ashore to dry out and brush their hair. Unseen by them, the
writer listens intently to their conversation from behind a convenient
rock, expecting to have his knowledge of girlish behavior soon
confirmed. Instead, for several hours before the hair brushing ritual
finally begins, the young ladies nap and read and talk very little. Then
comes the blatant O. Henry twist: one of them laughs and asks the
other if she has any burning desire to lay bare her soul, mentioning
the well known notion in books that girls always exchange deepest
confidences during hair brushing episodes. Her companion laughs
back and agrees to the sheer absurdity of such a concept, wondering
"how the idea started."

What else is left but rueful cuteness, a laborious anti-climax? After
the girls depart, Errington proclaims the mechanical truth of truism:

"Well," he announced solemnly to the horizon. "I got material and insight
anyway—even if they weren't of the kind I expected." Then he made a
bonfire of his story.

Unfortunately, the vision of literature unconsciously illuminated
here, who writes it, what it deals with, how it works, is as sophomoric
as the story itself. Surface is what seems to matter, surface details,

surface plot patterns, and there is not sufficient satire present to rescue style from vapidness.

More efficient and entertaining is "Mr. Percival Poynton and a Pig," the longest story Crapsey ever assayed, and one better fitted to her modest but genuine talent for narrow social comedy.[12] Caricature still prevails, but this time there is also an attempt, however feeble, to interject political satire as well. The Percival Poynton of the title is a young, stiff-necked prig from the upper classes who has come to Assaria, a small town in Kansas, to manage his widowed aunt's estate and engage in some law practice. As his name indicates, he is the epitome of stereotyped snobbishness, whom Edward Elliot, his friend from the East, characterizes as "the sort of a good fellow who makes it necessary for you to remind yourself every once in a while that he is a good fellow."

Percival has involved himself in local politics and is running for mayor as a reform candidate against Michael Finnegan, a saloon keeper who speaks with a deep brogue—a detail which Crapsey handles well. The socio-cultural distinctions and division are clean, clear, simple, even simplistic, if not too distant from the actualities of much local politics at the time.[13] Poynton personifies the inevitable reform movements that began among nativist factions (usually upper and upper middle-class) after immigrant groups, usually Irish, had taken control and inaugurated a self-perpetuating dynasty of corrupt bosses. He is weighted down with all the obvious defects and virtues of his kind: he is remote, humorless, prissy, condescending, honest, sincere, dedicated. His downfall—he has been established as a perfect comic foil from the start—is unavoidable, and is accomplished by the unwitting actions of a mischievious nephew and, ironically, his own friend Elliot.

Mr. Finnegan is conducting a raffle in his bar for a huge pig, the winner to be the person whose guess about the pig's weight comes closest to the actual poundage. While drunk the evening before a big debate between Poynton and Finnegan, Elliot has been mistaken by a new bartender for Poynton, and young Percy, the nephew, has slipped in and signed his own name to the list of guessers, a coincidence which seems to confirm the bartender's mistake. As a result, Finnegan gleefully reports to the local newspaper, whose editor resents Poynton's snobbishness, that Poynton had come into the bar himself, intoxicated, to guess the pig's weight, and that he has won. The debate—which Poynton mishandles, preaching down to his lower-class, largely Irish audience, asking them to throw out "the ignorant Irish element" and incurring wrath and derisive laughter—reaches a climax when Finnegan presents his opponent with his prize pig.

Interestingly, at the end, the humiliated Poynton refuses his aunt's offer to explain the mistake, realizing how wide the gap really is between Assaria and him. With "cold dignity" he asserts, "There will be no explanations—I shall leave Assaria to Finnegan." Reversal thus has an added twist. In a way, Crapsey has enabled him to win, has presented the town's people and Finnegan (and other Irish immigrants) in such a crude fashion that he appears superior, better off: our sympathy has returned to him, and to the native American *crême de la crême* he presumably represents. Perhaps comedy's demand for a happy resolution is responsible or perhaps Crapsey's own subconscious prejudices have slipped through, though in a light-hearted manner that does attest to her keen awareness of the then-current social scene. The portraits of Finnegan and his manager are warm-hearted but unfair in the extreme. There is scant doubt that their author feels most comfortable with and comforted by the cozy library and tea world of Poynton, an object of fun but an Anglo-Saxon repository of taste, education, refinement.

The story is easy to swallow, if again a bit obvious in contrivance, and does cover a broader canvas than the previous stories. It also maintains a cheerful air from beginning to end, with the plot unfolding rapidly enough to prevent fatal pauses. Its ultimate failure reflects Crapsey's personal limitations, her shallow conception of fiction as mere entertainment, a vision which leaves no room for subtleties of tone and character. Manichean extremes dominate too completely for anything but slapstick comedy to prevail.

The last short story Crapsey wrote for the *Miscellany*—or any other publication—was "Milord and Milady."[14] It is also the best story that she ever wrote, a romantic but well done melodrama that strives to cast some naturalistic light upon the stiff social poses and codes of behavior embodied by her two main characters, the Duke and Duchess of Glastongate, who are caught up in the coils of a stock triangle. Having always felt unloved, the middle-aged duchess has recently taken a lover, and is on the point of departing with him, abandoning her high estate and reputation in the process. In the past, the duke and duchess had invariably addressed one another with the formal "Milord" and "Milady" of the title, but this traumatic moment has resulted in second thoughts on the duke's part, a sudden sense of humanity and emotional loss. He calls his wife "Clarisse" and puts aside his normal reserve to profess his great hidden love for her, apologizing for a former lack of appreciation. Ironically, he had always most admired her coldness and control, the icy way in which she had lived up to the title bestowed upon her by marriage.

She, in turn, is now trapped too firmly in the "Milady" role for any last-minute salvation, and nothing her husband says can sway her from her decision, although she does chide him gently—softening somewhat under the influence of memories of the love-sick young girl she had once been—for not having "thought of this some years ago"; her words are a reference to his sudden passion, the specific warmth of his kiss on her hand. Regret dominates the scene, but Crapsey retains mystery, her sparse style aptly simulating the restrained life styles of her main characters.

The duchess rides off after promising (at her husband's urgent request) not to leave permanently until the next day. In the meantime, the duke has decided upon the ultimate sacrifice, realizing that he "loved her and she would never love him—again." He is determined to commit suicide to prevent her from losing her wealth and title, and does so with a duelling pistol. When his wife returns, she is stunned by the news of his uncharacteristic act of passion, asking to see the corpse. The subsequent climatic scene, and its familiar plot reversal, is done with a professional economy of effect:

They took her to the room and she stood alone by him, looking down into his face. "And you believed it?" she said. "You believed that I would—how could you?" There was no grief in her tone, no reproach, simply questioning. Then she spoke again. "Was it for me you did this—or the name? Perhaps for both." She leaned down as if to kiss him, then drew back, shaking her head. She laid the sheet over his face. "Both of us dead," she said, and went out of the room.

Irony triumphs, dictates terms, along with a proper coolness, and the closing refrain seems inevitable as the maid, when questioned as to whether the duchess wept or not, remarks, "Not a tear." Compression and sophisticated distancing have been manipulated with remarkable aplomb throughout, aiding the narrative's sardonic twists.

The simple power of "Milord and Milady" invites an important question: why did Crapsey not bring the same virtues to bear upon her poetry at the time? But poetry was, perhaps, still too exalted a concept, the elitist art that required gilded monuments for its realization, while the short story remained a method of civilized fun—a toy and plain tool.

None of Crapsey's stories are worth preserving in any strict critical sense, but they offer signs of a growing talent for literary technique—a talent which might have, if ever nourished by deeper feelings and commitment, established its author as a significant novelist.

III   Further Undergraduate Prose

Crapsey's other prose works from Vassar, including the various reviews she wrote for the *Miscellany* and "An Insane Episode"—the farce which appeared in the 1899 *Vassarion*—give evidence of the same lucid directness and economy of means. The books reviewed also provide some insight into what she was reading, and, more pertinently, what literary strengths she most valued.

Her first review was a consideration of *In Old Narragansett* by Alice Morse Earle, a popular historian who specialized in accounts of quaint customs from the past, usually the colonial past.[15] The book inspires Crapsey's boredom, though she compliments the author for her "very clever power of characterization" and "keen sense of humor." But, in summary, Crapsey must concede that the sketches and stories, however "well written in an easy, colloquial style," simply "do not make a great impression on the reader and even fail occasionally to hold his attention." The review is fair and to the point, even when dealing with material of a less than momentous nature.

The next review was not a review at all, but a commentary upon a collection of photographs of famous paintings which had lined Vassar's main hall since 1887, but which, Crapsey felt, were being neglected by students who seemed to pass them by without seeing them.[16] She realizes that no philistinism is involved, only the human tendency to take for granted (and thereby not **see**) the familiar, to miss what has become habitual. Never once, however, does Crapsey say how mere black and white photographs of paintings, despite the latter's deserved fame, could have much of an aesthetic impact. Behind her attention to photographs of Gericault's *Radeau de la Medusa,* Titian's *Flora,* and Delacroix's *Dante et Virgil* lies the unspoken but deep fidelity to Art with a capital A, Art as a polite social and intellectual ornament. This premise is crucial, because it constitutes the same rarefied attitude that was stifling her poetry. Of course the piece is well-intentioned, is sincere and goodnatured, but it also highlights Crapsey's vision of art as an educational rather than an existential experience. Her perspective illustrates the burden of her sex and her middle-class regard for order, which would congeal into an almost life-long addiction to form rather than content, to the scholar rather than the poet in herself.

But always literature intrigued her most; and the next book she reviewed, *Within the Hedge,* was a volume of charming but forgettable verse by Martha Gilbert Dickinson, one of the multitude of secondrate female versifiers who hid behind three names and threatened to blot out the authentic achievement of that earlier Dickinson.[17] What is prophetic about Crapsey's review, which is quite positive in the main, is the list of specific virtues she chooses to celebrate: "Miss Dickinson's success is largely due to her characteristic mode of expression, which combines an epigrammatic brevity with a subtlety and suggestiveness astonishing in the narrow limits she allows herself." Brevity, subtlety, suggestiveness, self-imposed narrow limits—these were the qualities absent from her own poetry at the time, although they were also destined to become the very qualities that would distinguish her writing after 1911, particularly in the cinquains.

Mrs. Dickinson, as the poem called "Fidelity" (quoted *in toto* by Crapsey) demonstrates, shared her reviewer's allegiance to Mandarin vocabularies—"hath" and "remembereth" are two examples—and to a penchant for imitations. Interestingly, Crapsey alludes in her review to a "criticism often heard of modern verse," which she identifies as sacrificing "sense to sound." It is clear that she regarded modern poetry as resting in the hands of Swinburne and his disciples, and that she had not yet read and/or accepted the French version of modernism as a neoClassic, Symbolist phenomenon, as elucidated in the writings of Rimbaud, Baudelaire, LaForgue, and others. But neither did she align herself with the popular line of nineteenth-century American verse, as personified in and handed down by Longfellow, which articulated a compelling urge toward moral strictures and neoRomantic structures. In a concluding paragraph, Crapsey chastises Mrs. Dickinson for "an over-fondness for interpreting symbols which may lead her into the habit of expounding texts in rhymed sermons." Preacher's daughter or not, Crapsey was, at least as a critic, rejecting didacticism early in her career.

Crapsey's next review was a paean of praise for Rudyard Kipling's tales of boarding school mischief, *Stalky & Co.,* which she felt called upon to defend against unnamed aesthete critics who had apparently been attacking Kipling's book for aiming at the masses instead of posterity.[18] She disposes of these critics with tart lightness, setting up straw men—one critic is depicted as shying away from the book's rough language, his "sensitive soul all in a shudder"—which she can easily demolish during the subsequent discussion of Kipling's virtues. Again, Crapsey comes down hard on the side of verbal economy and lucidity: "the stories are good examples of Kipling's heaven-sent gift for narration. In the simple telling of a story, the working out of it from start to finish, Kipling has few tales much superior to these." She could be writing about her own style in fiction, of course, although she is also suggesting that popular literature should be exempt from serious judgment because, unlike poetry, it entertains.

Her other remarks, including her description of the characters of the three boys in the story, seem equally just and sensible, if prosaic, but her slighting reference to their "lurid" language does intimate how cloistered her own (and her country's) view of fiction remained. Once more, the review's positive aspects are its commonsensical defense of popular taste and its associated ability to isolate the factors that made Kipling such an attractive figure for his age.

Crapsey's authentic skill as reader and critic were more advantageously displayed when she dealt with Tolstoy's *Resurrection*.[19] After an initial paragraph commenting upon Tolstoy's religious drive to replace the violence of human law with the "simple, clear, and practical" code contained in Christ's "Sermon on the Mount," she penetrates immediately to the heart of the novel, and, with short, crisp, carefully chosen sentences, describes its fundamental design and its primary failure as art:

The stupidity and corruption of Russian courts, the farce of trial by jury and the misery of prison life are set before us with terrible reality. Not a detail is spared or slurred over. The suffering and degredation and blind injustice of it all are pitiously shown. And yet, is the remedy which Tolstoy offers the right one? That is of course for the individual to decide. Most of us will find it hard to accept and most of us will not remember the social doctrines as the vital part of *Resurrection*. When we think of the book we will think first and foremost of the story of Demitri Nekhlúdoff and Katúsha Maslova. The purpose of the story in the book is of course to illustrate the doctrines shown therein. The course of it takes us into courts and prisons; shows us to individuals caught up in the "monstrous confusion of life" and tells of their fall and their resurrection. It is not however as illustrative of this or that doctrine that the story of Nekhlúdoff and Katúsha lives in one's memory. It stands by itself alone, separate from the rest of the book—one single, vivid, painful impression. If the book had been a novel, instead of only having a novel in it, what a marvelous one it would have been.

Pithy and cosmopolitan, these observations leave scant room for serious counterattack. The self-confidence of the review, its flat refusal to be overawed by Tolstoy's genius and past achievements, stimulates admiration. When, two paragraphs after these remarks, Crapsey attempts to pinpoint the Russian novelist's failure more concretely, she is in command. Describing the novel as "on the whole disappointing," she concludes, "It lacks unity. The interest is scattered and the effect of the whole is accordingly weakened. Tolstoy, whatever else he is, is not a master of the art of leaving out." Economy is again the yardstick of rebuke and praise.

Unfortunately, her personal load of commitments to obsolete aesthetic doctrines rarely led Crapsey to the heights attained by Tolstoy in his worst moments, and her next review of *Richard Yea-and-Nay*, an historical romance about Richard the Lion-Hearted by Maurice Hewlett, lends support to the view that Crapsey's very love of restraint probably hid an intense desire for the vaguer lushness of Romantic excess.[20] Though she ticks off Hewlett's faults with practiced accuracy and smoothness, denigrating his style as a "little too lovely" and his narrative as "over-dramatic with its machinery somewhat too evident," her emotions have obviously been stirred by the book's costumed sentimentality to the point of noncritical swoons. She goes on to define the style—despite its "hint of exaggeration"—as "exquisitely beautiful," ranking it above that of every other "present-day teller of stories," and also proclaims that the book's "whole conception and treatment place it beyond the ordinary." Her final sentence lapses into pure rhapsody: "Take it [sic] altogether *Richard Yea-and-Nay* is a book to read, to delight in, to remember." The extravagant praise for what can only be described as a mediocre, if slick, historical melodrama is another sign both of Crapsey's relative youth and of her loyalty to a superficial aesthetic in which "romance" is almost preRaphaelite in its self-indulgence—a further confirmation of the addiction for rhetoric that had marred and would further mar much of her poetry.

The last bit of prose that Crapsey contributed to the *Miscellany* was a sort of prose poem that was intended, apparently, to do nothing more than preserve, like a pressed rose, one "poetical" college experience. Written in her senior year, it has to be quoted in full for its decisive insight into the nascent artist who left Vassar in 1901:

A fleck of red in the tangle of green caught my eye. Separating the long grass with my fingers, I discovered a stalk of wild strawberries—the first of the year. They looked so exquisitely fresh and dainty, the four or five tiny scarlet globes bending their slender stem, that I hesitated to pick them. But a breath of their fragrance, faint and pungently sweet, decided me. I broke the stem and dropped the berries one by one into my mouth. They had a flavor of the woods and earth, a flavor that produced their own fragrance—sweet, pungent, evancescent. [21]

The style remains inviting, readable, and the author behind it ever well-intentioned. The brief episode itself, however, retains that greenhouse preciousness common to adolescent compositions. Also, the language lacks originality, sharpness; words such as "exquisitely" and "sweet" are in this context the flags of a lazy sensibility, and another reflection upon Crapsey's poetic failure.

A pleasant change of pace and format came with "An Insane Episode," which was labelled a "Prize Farce" when it appeared in the 1899 *Vassarion*. [22] It was the only time in her career that Crapsey attempted to deal with a dramatic mode, although the characters and plot line are not too different in degree and kind from the ones that dominated her short stories. Among the "Dramatis Personae," for instance, Mr. Gregory Wellington is listed as a young man "who knows all about girls," while his partner and fellow bicycle rider, Mr. Thomas Curtis, "is rather in awe of them." Besides them, the doctor, a nurse, and two patients—the scene is the Hudson River State Hospital, a mental institution located near Vassar—the two other characters involved are Vassar students, whose names also ring with Anglo-Saxon respectability, Miss Helen Raymond and Miss Alicia Wellington, Gregory's sister.

As in the short stories, the milieu is again chaste, intellectual, thoroughly upper middle-class. And yet "An Insane Episode" is far superior to the stories in its humor and plot manipulations. Even the young man's typically stilted speech configurations—those "Ye Gods!" and "By Jove!" exclamations Crapsey seemed to relish—suit the farcical ambiance created by the clever plot, which revolves around the mistake the two boys make initially, thinking the asylum is Vassar. They have come to give Wellington's sister a surprise party and, while standing in front of the asylum, discuss Vassar and the type of girl who must attend such a well-known school: to them, Vassar girls spend "all their time" studying, and are thus pictured as "all in spectacles and short skirts." Besides this in-group humor, the fun of the plot is supposed to emerge mainly from Wellington's vaunted knowledge about college girls, his boasted ability to identify them as to type, to "tell whether the jolly act will take her, or the serious or literary."

Naturally, Wellington then makes the error of categorizing the "Queen of Beauty," a harmless but attractive patient, as "the romantic, yearning, artistic type," and she leads him off on a walk through the grounds. Abandoned and somewhat apprehensive, the girl-shy Curtis is soon approached by a nurse in street clothes, and their conversation elaborates the basic error into another set of mistaken notions, including the nurse's funny description of a patient who believes that she is a golf ball, rolling down the hill and refusing to return until someone says "damn!" The story only reaffirms the young man's peculiar ideas about Vassar girls.

The final turn of the screw comes with Alicia's arrival. She has accompanied her friend Helen to the asylum as a favor, and Helen is taken on a tour of the place by a Doctor Stevens while Alicia, a bit nervously, waits alone outside for her return. As in most good farces—Wilde's delightful *The Importance of Being Earnest*, for example, which Crapsey may very well have read—the confusion multiplies towards a frantic climax. Warned earlier by Dr. Stevens about a wandering patient who is convinced he is Napoleon, Alicia, of course, believes that Curtis, just returning from his fruitless search for Wellington, is that inmate. The dialogue which ensues milks the situation dry, taking advantage of Wellington's name along the way, and is not resolved until Alicia's brother does reappear.

"An Insane Episode" is witty and inventive, as well as solidly constructed, and might work rather well in actual performance if the language were modernized. In fact, it was the finest thing that Crapsey had done at Vassar, perhaps because it tapped the fecund wellspring of comedy its author seemed to always have at her command, that gentle, perceptive sense of the absurd which illuminated her letters—and her life.

CHAPTER 3

A Study in English Metrics

IN her preface to the Knopf edition of *Verse*, Jean Webster wrote of her friend: "Adelaide Crapsey was, over a term of many years, an eager student of the technical aspects of English poetry." To completely understand Crapsey's poetry, that is, to understand her basic approach to the demands of a craft she had always admired above all others, it is thus necessary to realize that she did devote the lion's share of her energy—which was in increasingly short supply as her illness progressed—to analyzing, interpreting, thinking and writing about the nature of prosody, of English prosody. Indeed, as Professor Smith has observed, Crapsey "turned to poetry" only when "forbidden to continue with her metrical studies."[1]

The concentration on poetry began during her sojourn at the Saranac Lake sanatorium in late 1913 and early 1914, when her doctors became convinced that her weakened condition could no longer tolerate the constant, tedious syllable-and-accent-counting essential to her scholarly task. Dr. Baldwin, her favorite physician, remembered how she reacted with vehement protests to both the idea of not returning to Smith to teach and the need to abandon her grand metrical project, recalling that she "only wanted to pursue her studies of metrics."[2]

I *Origins and Materials*

There seems to be general agreement that Crapsey's serious work on English prosody began sometime in 1902 during her tenure at Kemper Hall, although the carefully crafted poetry from her college days certainly suggests that she had always been drawn to the technical side of poetic expression. It was Milton, her favorite poet, who was responsible for her decision to devote her scholastic career to a study of the relationship between accent and phonetics. She regarded the first line of his "Lycidas" as "purest poetry" and was particularly fascinated by the way in which the entire poem manipulated its vowels for lyrical effect.[3]

The immediate result had been an even more intense reading of Milton's major works and a determination to view his achievement from the perspective of the connection between his vocabulary—vocabulary as crucial syllabic, accentual choices, not as extensions of meaning—and his often subtle, ever masterful metrical system. From this emerged a further desire to compare Milton's prosody with that of a neoClassical offspring, Alexander Pope, and then to balance both against more contemporary figures, such as Tennyson and Francis Thompson. Ultimately, Crapsey would also realize the wisdom of providing some sort of basic model for the sake of broader comparison, settling upon the idea of analyzing numerous English nursery rhymes as well.

From 1902 to roughly the middle of 1913, Crapsey relentlessly pursued her metrical "thesis," which involved counting syllables from many long poems, drawing up charts, reading related technical texts, and organizing a mass of raw data to conform with accepted scholarly practice. Her mind responded readily to the somewhat monotonous tasks, perhaps reassured by the sense of security and purpose it engendered, the sense of snug dedication every scholar feels while intent upon a mechanical piece of research. And when she wrote from the sanatorium about "the favorite literature," she was making reference to her metrical studies, not her own cinquains.[4]

Her plan or thesis, which she had always identified as "her serious life work," was an ambitious one. It entailed an almost monumental attempt to isolate and describe how a number of major poets—major to her and most of her generation—solved key problems of metrical intricacy in a language where metrical feet and stress patterns had to contend with opposing structures of word-sense units, especially in polysyllabic constructs. In simpler terms, Crapsey hoped to be able to demonstrate the fundamental relationship between a poet's vocabulary and his prosody by analyzing the syllabic configurations of the poems chosen for study. She also apparently hoped to take advantage of her own research to write "a series of essays in criticism" in which technique could be more closely tied to the innate limitations of a language where monodissyllabic words had to prevail in any poem of length and metrical complexity.[5]

At Kemper Hall and later at Smith, Crapsey worked studiously upon her project, becoming known as something of an isolate in the process.[6] But it was in London, probably spurred on by the knowledge of her worsening health, that she made a Herculean effort to bring her massive research to a head, spending countless days in the British Museum's reading room poring over the required verse collections and numerous ancillary texts during 1910 and the early part of 1911. She had been encouraged in her work by T. S. Omond, the English prosodist whose own labors in the field of phonetic analysis she so admired; in a letter home dated May 24, 1910, she write enthusiastically about a letter from Mr. Omond advising her to submit an abbreviated version of her research to the *Modern Language Review* for possible publication.[7]

As with her poetry, Crapsey would not live to see any of her metrical material in print. Her reading program at the British Museum, however, is intriguing for what it implies about ultimate scholastic goals, much wider goals than those actually articulated by the incomplete manuscript left behind at her death. Besides studying the poets she proposed to use for her thesis, and many other writers like Keats, Landor, and Wilde, whom she simply enjoyed for their own sake, she read intently in related areas, consulting books and articles on metrics and English prosody, such as Liddell's *Scientific Study of English Poetry*, George Saintsbury's two volumes on the same subject, and, most important, Robert Bridge's analysis of Milton's prosody.[8] She also sampled more speculative material from the less precise field of aesthetics, looking into works by Croce and Santayana, among others.

Crapsey was obviously conscious of the need, however unclearly visualized, to shift her narrow technical focus from the area of syllabics to the larger problem of aesthetic choices as they reflect upon meaning and technique, which might have reached fruition in that series of critical essays she had intended to write. Interestingly, she also studied Schmidt's *Introduction to Rhythmics and Metrics to Classical Languages IV* and called for Goodwin's classic, *Greek Grammar*, which suggests that she was aware of the central problem in English prosody of distinguishing between stress and sound duration when considering syllabic patterns. She knew Latin, of course, and perhaps wished to see how a consideration of Latin and Greek—where prosody depends upon sound duration, not accent, for metrical structure—might help in understanding the tenuous relationship in English poetry between stress arrangements and the more natural accentual configurations conveyed through word length, where duration also plays a role. Crapsey's own careful use of pauses in much of her poetry seems to support such an interpretation.

But most of this must remain tentative and conjectural, since Crapsey's essays were never composed or outlined. *A Study in English Metrics* was published in 1918 and accurately characterized by Jean Webster as only "two-thirds" complete,[9] despite Claude Bragdon's reference to it as "an exhaustive scientific thesis relating to accent."[10]

II *Partial Conclusions*

A Study in English Metrics makes curious reading today, not solely because of its unfinished state, but also for the odd lack of real substance in what is finished. Even that portion of the study deemed whole, the first seventy-two pages, seems so narrow in choice of examples and avowed aims as to give the impression of willful pedantry. In her "Introduction" to the volume, Esther Lowenthal notes the completeness of this section and identifies it vaguely as assaying "an investigation of certain problems in verse structure," which is, unfortunately, as good a definition as any.

At the beginning, as if presenting a doctoral dissertation, Crapsey offers a "Synopsis" that attempts to outline the general nature of her undertaking, defining her "main thesis" as "an important application of phonetics to metrical problems in the study of phonetic word-structure."[11] A "sub-thesis" provides a distillation of her research results, which had led to a classification of poetic vocabularies according to their "distinct structural differentiation," a classification into three main types on the basis of their use of monodissyllabic (one or two syllable) words, as opposed to the less frequent polysyllabic ones. The first category would thus include poems where monodissyllabic words prevail almost to the exclusion of polysyllabic configurations—the latter running from zero per cent to a high of two per cent. The middle category allows for a polysyllabic range of from three per cent to roughly five and a half per cent, while the third would extend to a peak between seven and eight and a half. The rest of the first section goes on to analyze one hundred and twenty-five nursery rhymes, Milton's *Paradise Lost* and *Samson Agonistes,* and five of Pope's major poems—"Essay on Criticism," "The Rape of the Lock," "Elegy—Unfortunate Lady," "Essay on Man, I-IV," and "Epistle to Dr. Arbuthnot"—according to the three categories.

The results are tabulated in percentages related to the total number of words used in each poem, then added up for a statistical profile of each poet. Taken as a whole, the nursery rhymes show an

almost ninety-eight per cent use of monodissyllabics, but the tables
on the works by Milton and Pope indicate "a characteristic occurrence of polysyllables in Milton's poems running from about 7% to
about 8½%, with a tendency to drop toward 6% and to rise to 9%, and
a characteristic occurrence in the poems by Pope running from about
4% to about 5½%" (20-21). For Crapsey, the figures meant verifica-
tion of her three categories, firm statistical proof for her assumption
that the nursery rhymes would naturally tend to be monodissyllabic,
while the presence of polysyllabics would increase with the difficulty
of the poet, rising in percentages from Pope's work to Milton's.

But scientific methodology demanded further testing of her somewhat impressionistic scale, as she knew, and the next step was "to see
how far the scheme can be applied with reference to the vocabularies
of other poems" (22). Tennyson, Swinburne, Thompson, and
Maurice Hewlett are the subjects of the following four charts—
"always the selection of *whole* poems"—and they do indeed fall
neatly within the three categories: Tennyson, Swinburne, and
Hewlett occupy the "medium" grouping as exemplified by Pope's
verses, but Thompson's three works, "The Hound of Heaven," "An
Anthem of Earth," and "Sister Songs I and II," parallel the higher
polysyllabic range evident in Milton's poems.

The general results were surprising, at least to Crapsey, who had
expected to find a greater frequency of polysyllabic structures
overall. She was also surprised by the relative stability of her
categories, but her primary interest still lay with relating this
phenomenon to some sort of larger phonetic inquiry: "the more
intricate business of showing this proposition not in isolation but as
part of a consistent theory of English verse-structure as a whole" (29).

After briefly discussing a layman's vague approach to prosody after
the fact, that is, a scanning for mechanical feet, which is identified as
the practice of Saintsbury, and T. S. Omond's presumably superior
recognition of the complex relationship between rhythmic units and
syllabic structures or word units, Crapsey discusses the central
conflict between reading poetry simply as prose—reading it naturally
according to speech rhythms based upon word meaning and
syntax—and reading poetry as a pure metrical phenomenon, as an
arrangement of accentual feet. In the end, she sees the need to relate
word to foot, which provides justification for her tedious syllable
counting since that process had supplied the beginnings of a
mathematical (read *scientific*) approach to poetic vocabularies as
syllable constructs—syllables, not words per se, take the accents,

except in the case of most monosyllabics of course. Further, she returns to Saintsbury's *History of English Prosody* and *History of Prose Rhythm* to support her contention that poetry's fundamental distinction from prose might reside in its tendency to avoid having its metrical feet match words as units, forcing its rhythm away from the rhythm imposed by speech and prose patterns, which are word oriented. She then can move into a consideration of the material provided by her research results—elementary as they were—and note that in a poetic vocabulary like Milton's, where polysyllables are more common, "the longer word necessitates for its construction the use of a second accentual value, secondary word-accent" (47).

Such an observation, however, introduces another, deeper problem, "the problem of what for lack of a better term may be called the problem of weighting." Polysyllables, of course, involve variations in fullness of accent, while monosyllables—except for the articles—tend to be full or "heavy" by nature, and thus easier to manipulate and hear when part of a metrical scheme. Crapsey comes, at last, to the two elemental feet in English, duple and triple, which can be either rising (iambic and anapestic) or falling (trochaic and dactylic), and points out how an iambic foot can result in the secondary accent having to be read as full, if not a designed variant, while the anapestic foot permits the secondary accent to remain light, again if not a variant.

What this means in practical, critical terms Crapsey attempts to demonstrate by an allusion to the fairly popular view in prosody that progress was the governing factor in its history, that Tennyson's versification, for instance, represented a clear advance over and a development from Milton's. She denies this notion, since her research has shown that Milton was working with "a vocabulary of extreme structural complexity," which means that "his greater variety of word-forms imposes upon him all the difficulties of their manipulation, problems of weighting, of the management of the delicate, and treacherous, secondary accent syllables, and with these, since it is verse in duply rhythm, the question of variant feet" (63). From her perspective, a much fairer comparison would have to encompass, technically at any rate, a comparison between Tennyson and, say, Pope or Swinburne, both of whom fell within the "medium" range of polysyllabic usage.

The more general conclusion that Crapsey draws is that her admittedly "primitive" investigations suggest that "the historical development of triple rhythms in English poetry" must be reevaluated. Such a reevaluation, for example, could lead to the realization that Swinburne, who had often been complimented for the complexity and sophistication of his versification, was actually working inside very limited boundaries, that "we find in him not a highly developed but an early technique" (68). The delicious irony, for Crapsey, had to be that "the great main line of development in English poetry towards a mastery of triple rhythms" had already been accomplished by her beloved Milton in the *Samson* choruses.

But Crapsey brings the first section of her study to a close with a disclaimer, typically modest, that technical discussions of this type are concerned with isolating and defining elementary differences, not with making larger value judgments in "absolute terms of better and worse."

The second half of *A Study in English Metrics* (pp. 73-80) contains little more than a brief outline of Crapsey's intentions and another series of charts, which had been prepared to "present a portion of the data which had been collected for a second part of the study" (5). Her original hope was to probe deeper into the whole question of secondary accents by refining her categories further, until they could portray mathematical differences between monosyllables and dissyllables as separate groups, and between dissyllables themselves on an accentual basis. Under the heading of "Additional Analysis," her charts lead into the summary statement that "it is probable that of the whole number of words in any English poem, at least 70% are monosyllables" (75). But the charts stand out like fragments of a skeleton, since she did not have the opportunity to translate them into any meaningful, organic hypothesis or to flesh them out for purposes of relevant literary criticism.

III *Significance*

The profound limitations of Crapsey's aborted metrical study are obvious enough, and it is saddening to admit that so much of the laborious syllable counting could be done in a fraction of the time and effort today by computer. Her charts are valuable and do provide a number of tantalizing possibilities for other researchers to follow up, but it is only in a few of her general conclusions—e.g., her observation about Milton's metric superiority over much vaunted contemporaries of hers like Swinburne and Tennyson—that Crapsey's *A Study in English Metrics* retains a measure of solid historical worth. But subsequent investigations into the difficult and important area of secondary accents—the entire subject of stress-weight ("weighting")—renders obsolete many of her concerns.

And yet, for herself and her art, the study must have helped her to realize that stress rather than feet can be the sole measure of a line, and that insight no doubt aided her progress toward the blank verse diction of the cinquain. Also, if nothing else, her charts and monotonous syllable counting had abetted a growing appreciation of the relationship between natural speech and poetic diction, since the former invariably projects a rough iambic measure in English where stress beats per line (word oriented), not feet *per se,* provide the essential rhythm. The evolution of her poetic ear, in other words, was linked to her constant devotion to the metrical examples of admired models like Milton and Thompson, scholarship sparking creativity.

More to the point, poems such as "To the Dead in the Grave-Yard Under My Window," "Lines Addressed to My Left Lung," and a few others from the late period that simulate prose rhythms or conversational directness might be seen as reflections of her study's discoveries about the nature of accent as a function of prose as well as poetry, as an extension of meaning (word oriented) rather than an imposition of abstract patterns.

CHAPTER 4

The Early Poems (Before 1911)

JOHN Keats once observed that "in the very temple of Delight/ Veiled Melancholy has her sovran shrine," and this Keatsian melancholy must have claimed Adelaide Crapsey's secret heart for much of her short life, though it was assiduously hidden from public view, perhaps from herself at times—the "temple of Delight" seemed a more compatible and acceptable dwelling. The paradox of human nature at the core of Keats's insight in "Ode on Melancholy" defines the nature of the tension that underlay her aesthetic, but her early poetry refused to confront its negative dynamic, except in disguised form. More important, that poetry came slowly, at irregular intervals, almost reluctantly, and much of it was destroyed, since it was occasional verse.[1]

In the ten years between her graduation from Vassar in 1901 and the invention of the cinquain in 1911—the latter coinciding with a sudden worsening of her disease—Crapsey did not even think of herself as a poet in any formal, committed sense, did not submit her work for publication anywhere, and devoted a major portion of her spare time instead to her futile labors over English metrics. Regarding teaching as her profession and herself as a scholar in its ranks, she took and gave most pleasure in the daily chores associated with this view—students and colleagues alike well remembered her dedication and reserved good humor in the classroom.[2] Medora Hutter, a student of Crapsey's at Miss Lowe's, wrote decades later about her former instructor's "most contagious smile" and recalled that she "was an inspiring teacher—especially on her favorite subjects of poetry and prosody."[3] Having always relished both athletics and scholarship, Crapsey pursued life with an unremitting intellectual, emotional, and physical intensity, an intensity undoubtedly urged along by desperation as she realized that her life (and her grand scheme to supply a thorough study of English metrics) was foredoomed to incompleteness. As Rev. Crapsey sadly noted soon
54

after his daughter's death, "For fifteen years she had been a sick woman doing the work of two well women."[4]

If concentrated on poetry alone, this kind of almost compulsive energy might have culminated in Crapsey's locating and exploiting her own voice much earlier than she did. But the heavy demands of a self-imposed scholarship, as well as her natural optimism about the gravity of her illness, prevented most of the poetry known to come before 1911 from ever achieving true distinction. Too often, the poems are victims of undigested influences and a strained, archaic diction, subject to their conscientious author's concern with technique, with form over content, although several of them, notably the elegies for beloved literary idols, "John Keats" and "To Walter Savage Landon," demonstrate a surprisingly mature ability to mate compression with power.

I *Vers Libre and Keats*

One of the principal hindrances to dealing with Crapsey's early work is the difficulty of establishing a firm chronological pattern. She rarely dated her poems or talked about them much in the surviving letters. As a result, internal evidence usually has to suffice. Perhaps the best procedure is to treat the poems as groups or clusters according to obvious influences—e.g., Keats or the Georgians— relying upon clearly dated poems—such as the two elegies already mentioned and poems like "Expenses," "The Elgin Marbles," "Birth Moment," and others which are touched upon in letters or can be patently tied to a particular time and place—to act as anchors for the rest.

The earliest available verses, excluding those from Vassar, belong to 1905, a year which Crapsey spent largely in Rome, and include "Birth-Moment" (63-65) and "The Mother Exultant" (65-68), the two poems eventually chosen by the poet to commence her volume of *Verse*. They are fascinating, uncharacteristic attempts at *vers libre*, and especially uncharacteristic in their technical freedom and length. Like "Song of Choice" (120-22), which cannot be dated with any accuracy from external sources, they seem to have resulted from a deliberate attempt on Crapsey's part to go against the grain of her own predilection for brevity and strict versification, reflecting, perhaps, the influence of the nineteenth-century French Symbolists. Rimbaud's brave cry, *"Il faut être absolument moderne!,"* had apparently penetrated her young mind to the extent that she felt the need for experiment. Interestingly, it was the French, not Whitman, who supplied the impetus for her experiment, as it would for the founders of Imagism, T. E. Hulme and F. S. Flint.

But none of these three poems is successful, and their failure relates directly to the fact that their young author was not comfortable with the vague demands of free verse, where discipline must be constantly self-constructed rather than imported from the past. Furthermore, they are welded to the same disastrous taste for archaic language and concept evident in all of Crapsey's early verse. Francis Thompson should perhaps shoulder some of the blame. He seems to have been a persistent influence upon her early poetry—"Birth-Moment" is a rapid-paced allegory that probably owed much to him. His own Catholic love for allegory and intensely Romantic metaphors—more in the vein of Shelley rather than Keats, however—spoke directly to her taste for the same. His desperate search for religious salvation amid a life filled with drugs and advancing tuberculosis must have also awakened a strong sense of empathy.[5]

In "Birth-Moment," the central figure of a young girl emerging from the ocean to race toward life represents the birth of both sexual desire and romantic love, "Desire new-born," and "Desire on first fulfillment's radiant edge." The sexual passion behind the young girl's flight from sea to shore is explicit, if unelaborated; she is driven by a "Need" that is "uncomprehended but most deep divined." Though "virginal dear and bright," she is depicted as destined to wed nature—"summer skies at noon," "green fields," and "stars"—while becoming a "wanton mistress to the veering winds." She will also enjoy a pregnancy—"And new creation start"—that is literal and allegorical, a physical consequence of passion and art's nascence. The third stanza, which concentrates upon the "breathless space between" desire and fruition, describes it oddly as "dark-hidden, chaotic-formative, unpersonal," the womb idea being buried under prosaic, textbook adjectives; but the notion does lead into the stronger fourth stanza, set in parenthesis, dealing with a more personal interpretation of that moment "Before the mouth upturned and mouth/ down-dropped/ Shall meet and make the kiss."

The rest of the poem tries to connect the allegorical figure more closely with the voice of the human persona, who is envisioned as deeply in love: "Even so longing-swift/ I run to your receiving arms." The shrill, unconvincing climax makes the union total:

> O Aphrodite!
> O Aphrodite, hear!
> Hear my wrung cry flame upward
>   poignant-glad . . .
> This is my time for me.
> I too am young!
> I too am all of love!

The awkward language, the clichaic images, the peculiar insistence upon ill-mated compounds, all contribute to the poem's ultimate inability to "flame upward" into a genuine poetic experience. But from an historical perspective, "Birth-Moment" has the pathos of the poet's biography behind it, her own secret longings for normality and sexual love, as well as a certain skill at generating narrative movement.

Crapsey never married, of course, although she did have one or two fairly close male friends. There is a flirtatious letter, preserved by her mother, to her from a P. H. Savage, dated February 6, 1899, which includes a charming poem he wrote called "What are the eyes of Adelaide?" apparently in response to a note from the poet.[6] Also, Professor Smith alludes to a seemingly Platonic relationship Crapsey had with James Holly Hanford (1882-1969), a product of the University of Rochester, who graduated in 1904 and who taught briefly at a Rochester high school before going on to become a Milton scholar—Milton, Crapsey's favorite, drew them together, as did an interest in prosody.[7] In light of her nurturing era and family background, Crapsey presumably died a virgin.

"The Mother Exultant," a corollary to "Birth-Moment" and concerned with another topic remote from Crapsey's personal existence, depends upon a different fusion of allegory and reality: the narrator is a new mother who is celebrating "the hour of the vintage," which equates the grape harvest to the birth of a son as symbolic aspects of creation in general. A dual narrative scheme prevails again, and in the second stanza the mother explains to her infant son about the grapes and their journey from "the womb of the earth" to "the hands of the vintagers." She turns in the next stanza to her own story, revealing (to the reader at least) that she is the Virgin Mary and he Christ: "I was a maid and alone/ When, behold, there came to me a vision;/ My heart cried out within me,/ And the voice was the voice of God." This is a return, then, to the pious didacticism of "Hail Mary!"

As religious fable, "The Mother Exultant" revels in its biblical extravagances and its dependence upon stereotypes: "The vintagers laugh in the sun, / They sing while they gather the grapes." But, lacking even the intimation of sexual under-currents present in "Birth-Moment," it fails to escape the narrow pulpit drone of its own impulse toward coy parable making, and its final image could be a verbal mirror for one of Delacroix's lush paintings:

> Joy! Joy! Joy!
> The hills are glad,
> The valleys re-echo with merriment,
> In my heart is the sound of laughter,
> And my feet dance to the time of it;
> Oh, little son, carried light on my shoulder,
> Let us go laughing and dancing through the live days,
> For this is the hour of the vintage,
> When man gathereth for himself the fruits
>   of the vineyard.

In contrast, the allegory at the center of "The Song of Choice" has a pagan, almost medieval flavor, although its resolution insists upon a pseudoreligious decision. The principal dilemma is quickly sketched in the first stanza, which emits a delicate, risqué aura: "The maiden sat enthroned on the throne of her maidenhood: / There were two lovers that came to her to win her, / And one lover brought gift of red poppies, / And the other carried a sheaf of white poppies in his arms." Imagery is again the weakest link in the poem's narrative chain, as the two lovers make their pitches in alternating speeches, each speech relating the poppies to admirable attributes, physical and spiritual, possessed by the royal maiden. The red poppies, for instance, are proclaimed as perfect for making a wreath to adorn her hair, which is "golden and long" of course, soft as "cast shadows" (a felicitous touch), as "the path of the sun's light on the sea"; and the white ones suit "the still white thought of holiness/ That stirred in your soul when you awoke alone at dawn."

Unrequited lust is at war with the intangible beauty of virginity, of abstinence and religious devotion. To stimulate dramatic tension, which any long narrative requires, Crapsey has the maiden leaning toward the lover with the red poppies through most of "The Song of Choice," giving him the best, most daring lines: "Hold my red poppies between your breasts. / Your breasts are lovely and white/ And colour against colour it shall be as blood upon snow." As the persona finds herself longing "for the red poppies to hold them between her breasts," that sense of repressed sexual passion evident in "Birth-Moment" surfaces again. But Christian ethics demand virtue's triumph, and the maiden rejects erotic pleasures of the flesh, which cry out in her "to be accomplish'd," in favor of the spirit, "a bride-wreath of white poppies," and a lover who only kisses "the sleeve of her garment that is/ white as the wings of white doves."

Part of the problem with these poems is their heavy reliance upon standard sources—Francis Thompson, the Bible, ballads, and so on—for verbal, metaphoric, and thematic material, and Crapsey's incapacity (or conscious refusal) to deal more honestly with the emotional storms that must have torn at her inner landscape from time to time. Like the sunny, extroverted personality used in fighting off fears instigated by her illness, her poems never assay any candid treatment of inevitable, deeper, human ambiguities. As a result, as these three works indicate, true passion is not only rejected by her poetic characters, it is banished from the poetry altogether. The consequences are artifices too shallow to maintain reader interest. Perhaps such failure was unavoidable with the *vers libre* approach, as "John Keats" (68-69), not in free verse, might tend to prove.

This elegy for the poet who meant so much to Crapsey, written in Rome in 1909, bears the subtitle "February 1820-February 1821," bracketing Keats's final year of suffering. It is a relaxed, almost conversational poem, despite the presence of familiar anachronisms—"Thou," "thy," "Yea," "Lo," and so on—and attains several moments of intensity that are rare in the early verses. Religious precepts are absent, aiding the work's modernity. Authentic emotions such as grief, empathy, and self pity are handled with an impressive directness that provides the power so lacking in the contemporaneous "Birth-Moment," "The Mother Exultant," and "The Song of Choice," transforming "John Keats" into a moving statement upon the universal dilemma of mortality.

As would be the case with the cinquains and several other later poems, contemplation of death hones Crapsey's rhetoric down to its naked bone edge: "With dumb, wide look/ Thou, impotent, dost feel/ Impotence creeping on/ Thy potent soul." The agonized race against time of a young poet has patently stirred Crapsey's sympathies to the point of Spartan bluntness in raising a monument to Keats's courageous struggle and, perhaps, her own hidden horror of a similar fate: "now, caught in/ The aghast and voiceless pain/ Of death, thyself doth watch/ Thyself becoming naught." There might also be here a debt to Catullus and his famous address to his dead brother's "voiceless ashes," which would also explain its unusual bluntness at times. Whatever the influences and despite the archaic language, a carefully structured rhyme and meter scheme—more a stress-syllabic pattern than a foot measure—moves the poem smoothly toward an elegy's necessary climax of transcendental reflection.

In this case, Crapsey finds solace in the grass that grows each spring in the cemetery where Keats lies with the other dead—"Grave-fellows in/ Green place"—and in the poetic achievement that has since metamorphosized his gravestone into a "marking monument" that was "built for you long, long,/ Ago when Caius Cestius died," which represents a clever fusion of literal fact with symbolic statement.

Besides Keats and Catullus, the poem obviously owes a debt to Robert Bridges for its versification—and perhaps to Gerard Manley Hopkins for its occasional daring thrust at linguistic oddness, such as its rare use of an unexpected adjective, "aghast," and a Shakespearian pun, "Grave-fellows." Of greater import, however, is the emotional impact, which was lacking in the *vers libre* exercises.

Unfortunately, the three other poems composed around what could be designated as Keatsian themes, "Endymion," "Autumn," and "The Elgin Marbles," do not maintain the same level of performance. The last named was written in London sometime in 1910, when Crapsey was spending so much time at the London Museum, and the other two probably came a bit earlier. "The Elgin Marbles" (105-06) is a quatrain:

> The clustered Gods, the marching lads,
>   The mighty-limbed, deep-bosomed Three,
> The shimmering grey-gold London fog . . .
>   I wish that Phidias could see!

In formal terms, it is well done. The initial two iambic lines are dramatically violated by the third line to reinforce the shift in time and idea from a description of the actual sculpture to the intrusion of an exterior reality, which is also an intrusion of the present tense into the past. And the return to the iambic in the final line for a summary thought reasserts the link between the poet and the sculptor whose work she admires.

Again, Keatsian compounds prevail, but "mighty-limbed" and "deep-bosomed" are too hackneyed to succeed, while "shimmering grey-gold" hardly does justice to London's famous fogs. Only the last line—a girlish exclamation—is viable, relating the sad sculptor's literal fate to the insights of art itself. "Autumn" (82), on the other hand, unaccountably included in *Verse*, retrogresses to the pastoral imitations of earlier years. It seems more influenced by Keats's "The Song of the Indian Maid" than by his "To Autumn" in that the first, and strongest, stanza is structured around the allegorical figure of Autumn as a maiden: "Fugitive, wistful,/ Pausing at edge of her going" to turn and lean "to the earth with ineffable/ Gesture." There is an Oriental charm in the pretty details of the maiden's poetic realization, her skies compared to Spring's and found wanting, "frailer/ Bloom than plum-bloom or almond/ Lies on her hillside," but scant originality, except in the next-to-last three lines, which take full advantage of fading silences: "Unforgettable touch of/ Fingers withdrawn . . . Pauses, lo/ Vanishes . . Fugitive, wistful . . ." These should have been the stanza's closing lines, but the poet insisted upon the dead weight of "Ah . . me . . Alas . ."

Indeed, the poem itself should have ended with "wistful" as a modest, if quaint, cyclical, nature piece, but a two-stanza dialogue then ensues between a pair of unnamed lovers: the "He" compares his "love's heart" to a "frail" and isolated flower growing "on the cliff's edge," forever beyond "man's reach, aloof, apart," while she reaffirms the wisdom of this supposed insight, "what faëry way he hath/ Who turneth dreaming into faith." Criticism seems almost superfluous under the circumstances, especially since the failure is the familiar one of borrowed material untransfigured by either a new perspective or modern diction.

"Endymion" (108), another quatrain, is not much better, but at least possesses the grace of brevity:

> "Let me be young," the Latmian shepherd prayed,
>   "And let me have on night-time hills long sleep;"
> Whom she of Cynthus saw, Heaven's crownéd maid,
>   And gave his youth and dreams her love to keep.

Clichés abound and, as usual, the imagery is too imitative to be anything more than a heavily refracted homage to the poet Crapsey loved above all others. As such, the poem is technically competent and can be viewed as another step toward the dynamic briefer forms that would engage her attention (and greater skill) after 1910.

II *The Landor Influence*

Besides Keats and, to a lesser extent, Thompson, Walter Savage
Landor is undoubtedly the poet who looms largest in Crapsey's early
verses, and she apparently felt for him the same sort of personal and
poetic attachment she had for Keats, although his long life in no way
paralleled her own. As with Keats, she visited Landor's former villa in
Italy at Fiesole and his grave in Florence's Protestant Cemetery. R.
H. Super's thorough biography of Landor makes clear, however, that
he shared very little of Crapsey's restraint, in life or literature, though
his potent quatrains and other short lyrics supplied perfect bridges
for her subsequent journey from Keats to the Orient.[8]

Crapsey's pilgrimage to Fiesole resulted in the elegy "To Walter
Savage Landor" (79), which was written there in 1909. It is yet
another quatrain, which certainly confirms Crapsey's affection for
Landor's own quatrains and briefer lyrics—she copied several into
her notebook—and which was moving her nearer to the concept of
the cinquain:

> Ah, Walter, where you lived I rue
>   These days come all too late for me;
> What matter if her eyes were blue
>   Whose rival is Persephone?

There is a clear personal note present, as in the elegy to Keats, which
adds vibrancy, immediacy, as does the lack of excessive rhetoric; the
unforced iambic line approaches speech. Thematically, the apparent
allusion to Landor's love, Ianthe, who served as inspiration for so
many of his better lyrics but married someone else, hints at a similar
romantic failure on Crapsey's part. It also implies that the light or day
(life itself) which Ianthe represented has dawned too late for the poet:
her persona is conscious of missed opportunities, though the anguish
is hardly monumental.

In "Expenses" (80) there emerges a similar sense of gentle rue, but
it is lightened considerably by that self-mocking, comic air Crapsey
was prone to use as a shield against her real woes. Another quatrain,
the poem had been written in London in 1910 and sent home in a
letter. At the time, Crapsey was living at the brink of poverty, but,
typically, made light of the matter and refused to concede the true
extent of her discomfort. Medora Hutter, the former pupil, dropped

by unexpectedly, finding her "in a rather dismal little flat in Ebary Street to which she had come from Rome. She was obviously ill but made little of her bad health, and her sense of humor was as refreshing as ever."[9]

The poem echoes Landor's tendency to dash off brief poems on the prosaic travails of daily life, including domestic squabbles, real and imagined slights, and the deaths of beloved pets, poems that were often, ironically, superior to his more solemn, weightier endeavors.[10] "Expenses" has the additional value of an appeal to a Classical background, which Landor would have appreciated, particularly since the poem itself derived from his own "Dirce":

> Little my lacking fortunes show
> For this to eat and that to wear;
> Yet laughing, Soul, and gaily go!
> An obol pays the Stygian fare.

The common deprivation lightly described in the first two lines shifts in the final two into a clever play upon the Greek myth of the River Styx, which all dead souls had to be ferried across after paying the boatman, Charon, with the two coins that friends or relatives had thoughtfully used to close their eyes. An obol is an ancient Greek coin, a small silver piece, and the poet is suggesting that she could, at least, afford that much, could, in other words, afford to die, although having great difficulty living. The bitterness is muted by whimsey, but "Expenses" paves the way for the more desolate vistas of the cinquains; the very choice of a Greek myth over a Christian one might intimate subconscious disenchantment, albeit of a minor sort.

The quatrain called "Adventure" (80) denies the existence of this bitterness with a kind of hymn to free will, to the broad horizons offered by "Sun and wind and beat of sea," and the hymnlike quality is reinforced by the strict *a-a-a-a* rhyme scheme. Its conclusion, however, marks a return to an adolescent optimism that achieves ironic depth only in biographic retrospect: "All the world was made for me!" Compare this to the quatrain pretentiously entitled "To Man Who Goes Seeking Immortality / Bidding Him Look Nearer Home" (96):

> Too far afield thy search. Nay, turn. Nay, turn.
> At thine own elbow potent Memory stands,

> Thy double, and eternity is cupped
> In the pale hollow of those ghostly hands.

The sentiment expressed is certainly one that Landor would have
found congenial enough; despite the many references to the afterlife
in his poetry, he was never convinced that immortality as a supernatural vision was a genuine alternative, turning more and more to
the figure of "Memory" for relief from advancing age. Crapsey's poem
itself achieves a certain lyric poignancy that concludes with a strong
image of Memory as another self, a ghostly alter ego holding out its
hands (as a Madonna statue might) to offer the only immortality
possible: the personal past. Again, there is a distinct unChristian
flavor to the enterprise, a denial of resurrection.

Yet another quatrain in the Landor mode, "Safe" (106), uses a
storm metaphor to reassert Crapsey's commitment to art as a form of
salvation from the threats of hostile reality:

> Force and bluster? Mighty threatenings?
> Scorn I lightly,—Not for these
> Tell me when shall great Orion
> Catch the flying Pleiades?

After the initial rejection of nature's wild outbreak, the poem looks to
the stars for symbols of what is genuinely important, more concerned
with the mythic drama revealed and preserved there than with
physical danger. The Pleiades, of course, are part of the constellation
Taurus (the bull), and Orion (the hunter) is frozen in eternal pursuit of
its configuration. Put simply, Crapsey's poem is stressing the primacy
of imagination over mere phenomena, which earns further support
from the subtle connection to Keats's moving sonnet "When I have
fears that I may cease to be" and its allusion to "night's starr'd face"
and "cloudy symbols of a high romance."

Fittingly, "The Immortal Residue," the last quatrain in the Landor
manner to be considered here, is subtitled "Inscription for my
verse," and was intended by Crapsey to act as *envoi* for her *Verse*
collection. Like Landor in "Finis," she was writing her own epitaph,
and, like him, she clearly insists upon the triumph of art over life:

> Wouldst thou find my ashes? Look
> In the pages of my book;
> And as these thy hand doth turn,
> Know here is my funeral urn.

Though undoubtedly written later than the other quatrains, this one maintains their familiar refusal of Christian alternatives and prophesizes modern poetry's continued progress from "art for art's sake" to art as a replacement for lost religious convictions. It also indicates that the "mauve decade" in England had a potent effect upon both Crapsey's private beliefs and her artistic stance—she had always been more open to European than to American influences— and that her isolation in the British Museum's reading room was physical, not spiritual.

III Fin de Siècle *Themes*

Professor Smith's research has shown that Crapsey, during her London stay, read heavily in Baudelaire, a major source of inspiration for England's "decadent" poets of the 1890s, and was especially drawn to the literature and art of Aubrey Beardsley.[11] And certain of her own poems have, along with a decided drift towards the kind of desolate secularism evident in the quatrains, an obvious debt for theme and atmosphere to Ernest Dowson, Lionel Johnson, and other Georgian poets, not to mention Oscar Wilde, who was most responsible for giving the "mauve decade" its exotic ethos. This influence is not too unusual, since these other artists did articulate and embody the logical, if excessive, culmination of the neoRomanticism practiced by Crapsey's two main idols, Keats and Landor.[12]

The three poems closest in subject and spirit to the English *fin de siècle* taste for lurid sentimentality are "Evil" (124), "La Morte" (124-25), and "Pierrot" (87), none of which can be dated from external sources. "Evil" uses the language of Oscar Wilde and Algernon Swinburne to create a female figure of absolute corruption, "A silent woman with strange eyes" who sits alone on "a royal massive throne/ Of smoothly polished malachite." But Crapsey is transparently uncomfortable with such excess, and the portrait of her spying persona as "Unpalpitant as heart of death" remains unconvincing, although the flow of gaudy adjectives is smooth and handled with skill. The climax—a separate two-line stanza—is too melodramatic for much impact: "I will go creeping softly in/ Her eyes are promises of sin."

Though imitative, "Evil" does exhibit a general efficency of means in bringing a Beardsley-like milieu to life, even in the absence of genuine perversion. But another poem, "The changed request" (133), which might be a playful spinoff from Keats's "La Belle Dame

sans Merci," as well as a tart comment upon the tendency of the
Georgians and French Symbolists to create and delight in female
configurations of emotional and ethical extremes, seems closer in
spirit to her own sensible, more humorous perspective; its subtitle
pleads in mocking French, "O que m'importe que tu sois sage / Sois
belle et sois triste," and its two stanzas dwell upon the unavoidable
conflict between romanticism and reality, between the illusions of
love and the prosaic demands of marriage.

In the first stanza, the "ardent lad" begs his beloved to "Be sad, be
beautiful," but "never a lesser thing," a situation that changes
dramatically in the next stanza, which describes the morning after,
after seduction and art, with the break of day and a humdrum return
to lesser needs and passions. Thus, "while the coffee steams," he and
his once fierce "ardour" now ask, "Good Lord, my dear—please
smile!" This is the Crapsey revealed in the letters, American to the
bone, sensible, pragmatic, full of sarcastic fun at the expense of any
extravagance, still committed more to technique than matter. Her
letters home during the London period refer frequently to financial
problems, tourist details of place, landladies and friends from
America, even touch upon the steady labors over her prosody
research, but never a single mention of poetry or the poets she was
reading.[13]

But that repressed or disguised side of her so enamored of Keats's
and Landor's Romantic strain was also enraptured by the lush
language and eroticism evinced by the leading writers of the 1890s,
recalling the suppressed passion evoked in "Birth-Moment" and
"The Song of Choice" earlier. Restraint might have characterized the
persona Crapsey projected in her life and letters, satisfying an
authentic self and projecting the public self that circumstances—
family and era and place—fashioned from birth, but no complex
human being is ever without alternate selves, contrary impulses
capable of manifesting a polar opposition, even if only through the
relatively "safe" methods of literature. The ivory frigate of American
Puritanism, after all, was often kept afloat by the darker undercurrent
of secret passions for the luxurious relief of sin, dragging corruption
(slavery, lust, hubris) in its wake, as is clear in Melville, Hawthorne,
Poe's short stories—the latter's "imp of the perverse" haunted the
fiction of nineteenth-century America. And Crapsey was not immune. In "La Morte," she appears to be laboring through the very
excesses "The changed request" had been satirizing.

Ernest Dowson and Lionel Johnson stand behind "La Morte," but once again it is a Beardsley world and character being limned. Death is personified as a decrepit whore, "vice grown old," and the first stanza delights in depicting her ruined facade, the "wisped grey hair," the "rough wrinkled cheeks," the whole "hideous slatten [sic] guise." The second stanza introduces a different note, however, accentuating the odd attraction death retains for mankind, the "strange concentrate glow" that emanates from her yet: "beauty mysteriously/ Present in scum blurred thin on stagnant/ ill-odoured pond." A Puritan revulsion certainly gives this stanza its power—the pond image is effective, if so uncharacteristic—as physical desire and grotesque death are linked in "Corpse-light of lust." And the allegorical climax offers the ultimate metaphor of war married to necrophiliac instinct: "Who kissed her pale stale lips would kiss/ ten thousand kisses/ sepulchered." The idea is well-developed, intelligently evolved, but a governing excess blunts its final blow. Death had not yet become personal enough for Crapsey to handle it with any authority or realism, and so she resorted to a peculiar combination of *fin de siècle* decadence and Christian parable making for her attack upon the innate unfairness of human mortality. Many of the style setting writers of the 1890s would themselves retreat from their aesthetics of extremism when death approached—usually into ritual-rich Roman Catholicism—denying their own past selves in the process.[14]

The Baroque shadows of Beardsley are central to "Evil" and "La Morte," of course, and in "Pierrot" (87) Crapsey worked directly from one of his famous drawings, "Death of Pierrot," which appeared originally in the *Savoy* magazine and which the artist himself thoughtfully captioned: "As the dawn broke, Pierrot fell into his last sleep. Then upon tip-toe, silently up the stairs, came the comedians Arlecchino, Pantaleone, il Dottore, and Columbin, who with much love carried away upon their shoulders, the white frocked clown of Bergamo; whither we know not."[15] The sentimentality of the scene and its caption had the added pathos of Beardsley's own rapid decline to enhance them for Crapsey, and his youthful demise from tuberculosis could have only increased his appeal, as it had Keats's and Thompson's.

As a serious poem, "Pierrot" is almost irrelevant, a rather adolescent exercise in verbalizing the obvious without commenting upon it, though the narrative—a familiar Crapsey strength—moves swiftly, depending upon dactylic strokes for emphatic speed. But the climatic stanza neither surprises nor provokes insight:

Pillowed high he lies
In his bed;
Listen Columbine.
"He is dead."
Oh, poor Pierrot.

Seemingly sincere, such a simplistic approach begs for a sardonic "So what?" rejoiner. More to the point, it suggests that the Baroque visions of the "decadents" (English and French) remained alien to Crapsey's mind and heart, that the chief significance of her brief flirtation with the "mauve decade" was the discovery of the need for sparseness in her own poetry.

IV   Miscellaneous Early Poems

The rest of the poems which can be assigned to Crapsey's early years are less easy to analyze in terms of direct influences, although all of them are characterized by a consistent predilection for the Romantic terrain explored by Poe, Keats, Landor, Thompson, and other nineteenth-century heirs of Coleridge and Wordworth. The language, imagery, and basic aims are the studied result of close reading experiences, careful, earnest compositions riddled with classical and Christian references and dedicated to a concept of lyric poetry as the studio expression of a well-educated but somewhat detached sensibility. Originality and passion rarely intrude, but the poet's craftsmanship shows a steady gain in control—scarcely unexpected in what must be regarded as necessary apprentice efforts.

Since influences are mixed and positive dating impossible, the poems have to be approached thematically. There emerges, for instance, an entire group of religious verses—"The Entombment" (82), "Grain Field" (86-87), "Harvesters' Song" (90), "Rose-Mary of the Angels" (90), "Cradle-Song" (95), "The Crucifixion" (97), "The Two Mothers" (122-23), "An Early Christian Hymn" (129), and "Traces of the Rustic in Amos" (131-32)—that depend upon the Bible for inspiration and are quite contrary to the "pagan" attraction that the Romantics and late Decadents held for Crapsey. In a way, they are a throwback to the pious didacticism exhibited by her college poems and remind the critic that she was the product of a country and a household, however liberal the latter, still firmly rooted in conventional Protestant myths and ethics.

None of these religious verses rise above the level of competent versification, but a few of them are worth noting for their prophetic concern with brevity and the less pleasant aspects of Christian allegory. Two of them in particular display a technical starkness that implies a further step toward the cinquain, a further modernity, though the situations and imagery are traditional. In "Grain Field," the sunny aura of a childish Sunday School recitation is cleverly utilized to accent the horror behind a handed-down myth:

> Scarlet the poppies
> Blue the corn-flowers,
> Golden the wheat.
> Gold for The Eternal:
> Blue for Our Lady:
> Red for the five
> Wounds of her Son.

The nursery rhyme neatness of this kind of poetic equation shifts in "The Entombment" into an epigram, is squeezed almost pun-dry:

> *In a cave born*
> (Mary said)
> *In a cave is*
> *My son buried.*

Aided by the title and hints at a Henry Vaughan "wit," the poem infers a relationship between womb and tomb, while providing a different slant upon the Christ-Madonna matrix. In fact, the focus upon Mary's anguish rather than the glory bestowed by the divinity of her offspring might portend a growing awareness of women's peculiar position in a man's world, anticipating the much later poem "The Witch." Also, expanding references perhaps beyond the pale of textual criticism, it could be said that Crapsey was probably interested in personalizing the inevitable sorrow of motherhood in a time and place where children often died early, as in the case of three of her own siblings.

The other religious poems are more flaccid and hackneyed in their realization, either settling for lyric prayer, as in "Rose-Mary of the Angels" and "An Early Christian Hymn," or relying too much upon a coy fable-like effect, as in "The Two Mothers," "Cradle-Song," and "Harvesters' Song." "Traces of the Rustic in Amos" is also guilty of the latter fault, but it at least possesses intimations of humor in its portrait of the Old Testament prophet as social outcast because of his lack of etiquette: "'Tis sad but true that Amos he/ Was less polite than ought to be/ A prophet though he is but minor."

Opposing the Christian trappings of these poems is another set of verses typically Romantic in their allegiance to classical figures, particularly "Hypnos, God of Sleep" (79), "The Fiddler" (111-13), "Narcissus" (84-85), "Cry of the Nymph to Eros" (94), and "To Anacreon" (130-31). "Narcissus" manages to achieve a degree of drama in its use of an offstage interrogator, who asks Narcissus what he sees in the pool, either the blue "Colour of Heaven/ Mirrored, repeated?" or the brown "Tree-trunks and branches/ Wavingly imaged?" His reply supplies the tension of a fate-heavy ambiguity: "Nay but mine eyes;/ Nay but the trouble/ Deep in mine eyes."

But Crapsey lacked the internal urgency at this juncture in her development to wield mythology as a scalpel for uncovering the deeper corridors of the human unconscious. Instead, she tended to blunt the harsher, sharper implications of her borrowed material, as in "The Fiddler," where she transforms the elemental myth of Orpheus into a fairy tale that studders with juvenile excess: "Hark you! It's night comes slipping in." The poem entitled "To Anacreon," which had been dedicated to the "long-lived (c. 568-478 B.C.) Greek lyric poet who wrote chiefly in praise of love and wine," [16] is a good example of this softening process in action.

Anacreon is consoled throughout for the cruel sorrows inflicted by a nymph who resisted his advances solely because of his age, "careless-mocking, took her flight/ Because for-sooth the snow of white/ Advancing age lay on the brow/ Of him who sang." Anachronisms continue to impede the progress of Crapsey's verse, as do the unoriginal images, while the technique seems intent upon preserving an obsolete formula, the formula of classical address overturned by Wordsworth a century earlier. Worse, the need to preach remains an encumbrance: "For him whose song-inspired hand/ Strikes tunefully the eternal lyre/ Of vibrant flaming-stringed desire,/ The day of bliss is never over;/ He is forever ardent lover." In "Cry of the Nymph to Eros," an authentic cry of despair struggles to surface, but is muffled by the archaic format that betrays its author's yearning for cathartic romance: "Hear thou my lamentation/ Eros, Aphrodite's son!/ My heart is broken and my days are done."

The theme that darts like a silver needle through most of Crapsey's early poetry is the tragedy of unrequited love and unfulfilled sexual passion, which were the very subjects least open to candid treatment in an age when American females, however intellectual, were firmly bound by the Victorian precepts governing the middle class's days and ways, when *Little Women* was still the unofficial text for girls on the brink of maturity. Such social restrictions, coupled with Crapsey's own inclination toward hiding behind elaborate Romantic masks in the Keatsian fashion, often wasted her modest talent upon a whimsical (as opposed to an ironical) retelling of inherited narratives that appears curiously adolescent—she was in her twenties when these poems were written. Besides the constant recourse to classical situations which were frequently reduced to fairy tale proportions, there were a number of instances where actual fairy tales furnished the plot, as in "Rapunzel" (84) and "The Golden Princess" (133).

The former has the advantage of Rapunzel being her own narrator, plus the restraint and casualness of a conversational form that permits Crapsey to use pauses (Dickinson's dashes translated into two periods) favored in her more natural letters. The last stanza achieves a quite modern sense of unease, of unspoken dread:

> She left at dawn . . I am blind
> In the tangle of my long hair . .
> Is it she? the witch? the witch?
> Ah, who is there?

But "The Golden Princess," a much less successful poem, lapses back into the dense, unconvincing language of an unrelieved stereotype: "Oh, gallant princess, soul and self sun's hue, / As heaven tender are thine eyes of blue."

Crapsey also continued to be influenced by French sources, and two poems, "Avis" (85-86) and "Aubade" (113), were designed as echoes of her reading in medieval literature. "Avis," which is a rough translation of "a French song of the 13th Century,"[17] presents another "fair" maiden who rises with dawn and finds "Five flowerets" which she knits into a "fragrant garland." The two lines of the climactic last stanza stumble into total absurdity: "Go thou from thence thy pity!/ Thou lov'st not me." But "Aubade" attempts pure song, although still tied to a "virgin" maiden bringing in dawn, and its failure is more inevitable: "The vision that came with gradual steps departeth in an instant;/ Hasten, lest it be unbeheld of your eyes." Of greater interest and merit is the untitled poem (123-24), written on the reverse side of the sheet containing "Aubade," in which familiar feelings of frustrated sexual desires find their voice: "I offer myself as wine graciously held in golden goblet/ A subtle drink of fire—" And yet the idea that a refusal of physical consummation is a "sin and bitter waste" is certainly pagan, not Christian, attesting, I believe, to Crapsey's ambiguity regarding the eternal conflict between flesh and the ethical demand for continence. As often as she placed her female projections on a Virgin Mary pedestal, just as often she hacked away at that pedestal with the ax of repressed lust.

Other poems from the period before 1911 emphasize Crapsey's willingness at times to leave herself open to somewhat less traditional approaches. A quotation from Shakespeare's *Hamlet*, for example, supplies the germ of "John-a-dreams" (110): "Yet I, / A dull and muddy-mettled rascal, speak / Like John-a-dreams, unpregnant of my cause, / And can say nothing!" Crapsey drives this into a religious parable of sorts, with "John-a-dreams" portrayed as an innocent bumpkin who is blessed by a complete lack of interest in worldly pursuits, a naif who, even if wandering accidentally into heaven, "needs he not to fear." It is too cute by far, too trite to succeed, but preserves a childlike tone that is appealing. This might have owed something to the pervasive influence of Emily Dickinson, and in "Non Solo" (129-30) Crapsey adopted her voice with almost undisguised faithfulness. Its final stanza defines its entirety:

> Oh, many things I do not know;
> It's rather nice to have it so.
> The Universe is heaps of fun
> If I can't say how it is run.

From a psychological standpoint, perhaps the most fascinating of the early poems is "There's a gay girl laughing" (127). Though not a strong poem by any means, it does contrast the polar selves which Crapsey must have labored long and hard to keep in balance: "a gay girl laughing / For pleasure of the day" as compared to "a woman very sorrowful / As empty days go by." The only resolution was the absence of one: "Who am I . . . Who am I . ." The answer, of course, lay in the future with the woman of sorrows, closer to the flat, brave, enigmatic notes of despair uttered by the cinquains and expanded in other late poems.

V   *General Conclusions*

Certain statements about the early poems are unavoidable. Lacking dates of composition for the most part, no precise chronological pattern can be established, but there seems to be a constant movement away from the Georgian school of excessive decoration or rhetorical flourishes toward a more natural, more compressed mode of expression, which would further buttress the conclusion that the shorter verses, such as "The Entombment" and the handful of quatrains discussed in this chapter, came later than most of the others. In addition, the general failure evident throughout this work appears directly connected to Crapsey's weak grasp of imagery, to her penchant for archaic disguises and inherited rhetoric, and to her overall refusal to deal candidly with negative emotions, unacceptable attitudes. Consequently, only those poems which approach the edge of genuine feeling, such as the elegies for Keats and Landor, ever approach true poetic intensity.

The voice that speaks loudest in the early poems is the odd voice of a professor of prosody who remains trapped inside a little girl (her younger self?), a voice divided against itself, unsure of the crucial relationship between Christian and Classical myths and the severe demands, emotional and intellectual, of a highly sophisticated and revealing art form. Too often, form dominates content to the point where the surface of the poem and its inner meaning are indistinguishable, equally simplistic, equally incapable of delivering complex insights. Another notable deficiency—a common nineteenth century American deficiency—stems from the imperative, rarely resisted urge to preach, despite a natural and intelligent adhorrence of such didacticism, and a parallel tendency to minimize the struggle between sexual desires and standard Christian dogma.

But none of these serious flaws can obscure the fact that Crapsey's early poems never cease attempting to discover their own ways and means, using whatever resources were available, including such diverse material as the Bible, Keats, Thompson, Landor, Dickinson, Poe, Baudelaire, fairy tales, medieval lyrics, French literature, and the alien, decadent, exotica served up by Beardsley, Swinburne, Johnson, and Dawson. And it was undoubtedly this willingness to remain open to contradictory outside forces that culminated in the invention of the cinquain.

Before 1911, Crapsey was indeed a child of her times, but, in summary, it might not be unfair to quote from Louise Bogan with respect to the special problem she had to confront simply because of her sexual identity, which tended, for a host of cultural reasons, to encourage continual allegiance to so many obsolete mannerisms: "it is apparently more difficult for women to throw off the more superficial fashions of any society in which they find themselves."[18]

CHAPTER 5

The Cinquain

ADELAIDE Crapsey suggested that she had invented the cinquain in 1911 by dating the ones included in *Verse* as all having been written between 1911 and 1913. But her biographer claims that she "actually developed the cinquain late in the summer of 1909 . . . although most of her cinquains were written between 1911 and 1914."[1] Whatever the case, the emergence of this unique short form—unique in English, unique in its metric makeup—also coincided with the intensification of the poet's disease and her confinement in a sanatorium. As a result, it seems to have been another example of a poet discovering both her voice and her obsession (death) in the same instant. The power so notable by its absence in the early works now came to the fore, expressing itself most forcefully through a highly demanding construct that perfectly suited Crapsey's well-developed interest in prosody.

I *Evolution of the Cinquain*

Thanks to the labors of several scholars, particularly Hideo Kawanami and Susan Sutton Smith, tracing the historical evolution of the cinquain is a relatively straightforward business. Perhaps the original impulse derived from Crapsey's admiration for Landor's shorter poems and her own frequent use of the quatrain, which she found congenial and fruitful. More important, during her last year in London her intense research in prosody had exposed her to a host of authors whose various styles undoubtedly encouraged the whole idea of experimenting in verse.

Like H. D., Ezra Pound, T. E. Hulme, and T. S. Flint, the early Imagists whose first literary home was England,[2] she perceived the need for a retreat from the rhetorical excesses associated with the Georgian poets, excesses of emotion as well as language. The neoClassic grace of understatement, which had always reflected Crapsey's personality and found favor in her few prose works, appeared essential as a pioneer method for exploring heightened states of consciousness not normally given to understatement. The cinquain, in other words, like the free verse products of Imagism, can be viewed simply as an almost inevitable backlash, a technical retrenchment after a period of extravagant assaults upon the Romantic heights.

More concretely, besides the obvious influence of Landor and the French quatrain—not to mention Emily Dickinson's mastery of concise lyrics—Crapsey was quite directly influenced by Japanese literature, anticipating Pound's movement in the same direction years later, and had also been reading translations of Chinese poetry as early as 1904 or 1905 in Rome.[3] She had no knowledge of the Japanese language, of course, and thus had to rely upon translations. As Dr. Kawanami has convincingly demonstrated, her major contact with Japanese literature, especially with the haiku and tonka forms, came through the French, through Michel Revon's *Anthologie de la Littérature Japonaise des Origines au XXe siecle*, which provided extensive discussions of Japanese techniques along with its numerous examples of haiku and tonka poems.[4] She had also read Yone Noguchi's collection of translations and original compositions based on Japanese forms in *From the Eastern Sea*,[5] and the library in the Crapsey home in Rochester boasted a copy of William N. Porter's English translation of *Hyaku nin isshiu (Single Verses by a Hundred People)*, an anthology of tonka dating back to 1235, which she probably consulted as well.[6]

Professor Smith has pointed out that the sole link between Porter's tonkas and the cinquain invented by Crapsey resides in their use of five lines, since they are a syllabic, rhymed form often rendered into uninspired English.[7] Noguchi's translations are not much better in terms of "creating" English poetry, but Crapsey did copy one of his translations from Basho into her notebook, which supplies a direct connection, at least, between her and his work.[8] The greatest debt, however, was to Revon, Crapsey having copied eleven tonka and eight haiku from his anthology, reworking several of them into her own cinquains.[9] She also copied some of Revon's notes on the haikus translated and was obviously interested in the haiku and tonka for more than just technical reasons, seemingly intrigued by their ability to juxtapose two contrary images—eternal vs. momentary, stillness vs. motion, and so on—in order to project a sudden, complete, frequently multitiered unit of poetic perception.

But Crapsey was concerned with sound *and* meter, which was not true for Revon, Noguchi, or Porter, and in her attempt to create an English parallel for Japanese forms she was striving to do more than outline a syllabic pattern. Because Japanese is not an accentual language, most translators are content to render its verses as strict syllabic and line schemes, so that the haiku, for instance, is usually regarded as a seventeen syllable unit of three lines (five, seven, five), while the tonka is thought of as a five-line construct with thirty-four syllables (three lines of six and two of eight but distributed arbitrarily). Crapsey, however, in concocting the form which she believed "to be the shortest and simplest possible in English verse,"[10] developed the cinquain as an unrhymed, five-lined structure based upon a rigid accentual pattern (one, two, three, four, one stresses) that had the effect of "working up to and falling away for a climax."[11] Although superficially following the tonka arrangement in English, Crapsey's cinquain is closer in spirit to the haiku—the haiku is the more concentrated and demanding of these two Japanese lyric forms. Professor Smith has rightly stressed the accentual nature of the cinquain, which had been previously noted by Louise Townsend Nicholl and Sister M. Edwardine O'Connor and which was confirmed by Crapsey's own use of stress marks in early versions of a few cinquains, but many "experts," including the prestigious *Princeton Encyclopedia of Poetry and Poetics*, have continued to view it as a syllabic arrangement (two, four, six, eight, two) and nothing more.[12] The sprung-rhythm effect of that last line alone, however, would tend to negate any such readings, and it is this effect which enables the previous four lines to retain their dynamic, progressive character.

As envisioned and used by its creator, the cinquain focuses a haiku's taut compression of emotion into a single striking symbol or metaphor, with the latter building toward a climax of severe but precise understatement that will trail off in the last line.[13] At a cinquain's conclusion, the movement of thought *and* form (and breath) is downward, outward, a release, sometimes explosive; but its climactic movement also reveals a sudden intellectual and emotional sense of linkage, of new completeness. Thus, in a formal way, the cinquain imitates the classic mystery tale, the build-up of tension being resolved or "solved" by the comprehension of the central metaphor offered in the next-to-last line.

II *The Cinquains in* Verse

The best way to comprehend the cinquain as an organic form is to analyze it in action, of course. Most of the cinquains Crapsey wrote were collected in *Verse*, which certainly suggests that she believed these twenty-nine most effectively carried out her concept.[14] But a critic more removed from their inspiration and actual composition cannot be so generous. Regardless of original intentions or the form's special nature, it is not too difficult to select the cinquains which seem to achieve a perfect blending of method and means: "November Night" (70), "Triad" (70), "The Guarded Wound" (73), "Night Winds" (73), "Amaze" (74), "Madness" (75), and "The Warning" (75). Though different critics might wish to include a few others, it is unlikely that they would exclude any of these.[15]

In a general way, like most literary thrusts into the unknown, these seven share a common emphasis upon what might be described as the dark aspects of human experience. "November Night" uses pauses and the paper's own vast white spaces to create a haunting vision of winter which makes death an openended reality:

> Listen . .
> With faint dry sound,
> Like steps of passing ghosts,
> The leaves, frost-crisp'd, break from the trees
> And fall.

The initial command (a trochee) establishes the hushed mood, aided by the pause of periods, while the second line (an iamb and spondee, though no single word takes a strong accent) amplifies the governing silence by its intrusion, and the third line, the first to insist upon a preconception, upon "ghosts," reverses the normal metaphorical order into image *preceding* literal object. The fourth and longest line completes the central simile, using the onomotopeia of "frost-crisp'd" (almost impossible to say rapidly, even without the fencing commas) to accentuate the conflict of sound *versus* eerie silence. The last line, which must be read as trailing off, back into silence, summarizes not what is actually happening, the falling winter leaves, but what is implied in the core mystery: what do the leaves represent, intimate?

The poem is atavistic in the manner in which it summons up an

awed, church-solemn response, and "November Night" does not
waste a single syllable doing it. Vowels dominate, except for that icy
"frost crisp'd," and smoothness aids the whispering atmosphere.
Thematically, the cinquain has provided a unified image or *gestalt* of
winter's portentious stillness, though dramatic values are introduced
and maintained by that first command, by the direct imposition of a
persona speaking aloud. This interpretation is open to contrary
speculation, to be sure, but the prevalent feeling is clear: like a good
haiku, "November Night" has offered a single instant of concentrated, fused image and though based upon two opposing realities
(implicit stillness broken by tumbling leaves), which leaves the
reader free to supply his own ramifications—these might involve
considerations of the entire poem as a harbinger of death or seeing
(hearing) in its stress on "ghosts" and breaking sounds the deaths of
others in the past.

"Triad," perhaps the best known of Crapsey's cinquains, appears
totally different in the method of achieving its power, though similar
in aim and equally successful at doing so. The speaker here takes a
more active, less tentative role, giving the impression of smug and
absolute completeness, of a closed experience:

> These be
> Three silent things:
> The falling snow . . the hour
> Before the dawn . . the mouth of one
> Just dead.

Like all metaphors, it is an equation of course, but not quite as closed
as it seems. The movement from snow to the hour *before* dawn
(traditional time of "darkest" expectations, of death) to the breathless
mouth of a corpse, from white to black to both conjoined, moves from
motion itself to a total absence of it, figuratively suggesting that
winter as death—the Romantic fallacy of nature reflecting a human
mood—is an inevitable balancing of polar forces, which must con-
clude in fatal, encapsulating stasis. But is it really? At poem's end, the
questions linger, multiply: why the hour before dawn? is it a birth
symbol? what corpse? who is speaking? And questions mitigate
against a closed system, intimate that the closure is more linguistic
than genuine, that language itself remains a sign of life, which could
mean that this poem represents a gesture of hardheaded survival, a
human, literary conquest of nature's indomitable laws.

Though personal, the poem has obvious links with Emily Dickinson hearing a fly buzz after death, refusing full grammatical stops, insisting upon yoking odd elements, hinting at immortality under the obsessive threat of dissolution. It also combines a sort of folk or fairytale syntax with vague echoes from traditional ballads. Further, the aura of mystery hovering over "November Night" and "Triad" would seem to be an essential element for Crapsey at her strongest, probably because it projects an openended form and poetic experience, despite the paradoxical rigidity of its format.

And the same aura emanates from "The Guarded Wound," even more intensely:

> If it
> Were lighter touch
> Than petal of flower resting
> On grass, oh still too heavy it were,
> Too heavy!

The title itself is open and remains so, as the rest of the poem merely describes one facet of its existence, symptom, not cause. Consequently, the reader is not just free to speculate on its meaning, he is forced to do so by the sheer magnitude of the pain being manifested. The immeasurable lightness of a flower petal lying on grass betrays a poetic extravagance that would be playful if the subject were not so tragic. As a "guarded" wound, title and poem suggest many possibilities for concealment, such as shame, horror, modesty, or convention, without demanding a biographical reading—the latter might theorize rejection by a lover. Also, the strong last line, stressed into a near shout, avoids the cinquain's usual lapse into silence, into entropy and anticlimax, making it more disturbing and dramatic than the other two.

Compare it with "Night Winds," where the question at the heart of the poem is literal:

> The old
> Old winds that blew
> When chaos was, what do
> They tell the clattered trees that I
> Should weep?

The landscape is a mirror of the harsh terrain in "November Night," but the hand behind the metaphor is somewhat heavier, more blatant. The term "chaos," for instance, possesses religious connotations, before God created earth and man, which is reinforced by the emphasis on the ancient quality of the winds—the end rhyming of "do" and "blew" (rare in the cinquains) adds to its effect—although the same feel for the impact of onomotopeia is present in "clattered." But the religious or biblical atmosphere does not violate the fertility of the question, coupling death with a moral condition but not insisting upon it. The solemn, unavoidable reply—all that is is temporal, including man himself—still leaves room for variant readings, such as envisioning it as a private death rattle or as a medieval lyric on seasonal devastation.

But the finest of Crapsey's poems in any form, "Amaze,"[16] is least open at first sight, personal poetry mated to the highly compressed world of haiku emblem:

> I know
> Not these my hands
> And yet I think there was
> A woman like me once had hands
> Like these.

Nature is excluded for a change, and a quiet, if dramatic, scene is hinted at, a woman staring at her own hands, an older woman contemplating older hands. They have grown alien to her, to her still-young mind, but she recognizes (in the climatic last two lines, where no "falling away" is in evidence) a great truth about those hands and herself: the lines of descent, perhaps, through mother and grandmother and back through a family tree or even the broader concept of a line of female descent down through the ages from Eve. The past and present have been fused into a single entity and event, brilliantly so, but at a more subtle level the persona is still alienated from her own hands and, by interpretive extension, her physical, aging self.

Winters views "Amaze" as encapsulating a powerful "hallucinatory" experience of impending death, but I think he is injecting biographical knowledge too easily. Reading into these poems from Crapsey's life can be unfair and counterproductive for a critic, though valuable at times for the purpose of describing the creative process itself. Yes, the poet was dying in a winter world, and, yes, this provided the energy for her obsession with death, which, in turn, fired her imagination to reach beyond itself; but what makes these cinquains potent is their universality. In isolation from the particular biography, they supply the heart of mystery that keeps literature alive, fullblooded, if not always sane.

The last two cinquains which can be numbered among Crapsey's total successes, "Madness" and "The Warning," are remarkably similar in exuding this same air of mystery, while never abandoning concrete experiences within a symbolic context. In "Madness," prickly herbs and bushes, echoing Christ's crown of thorns, are enumerated as discrete images, but finally knit into "Singing I wreathe my pretty wreath/ O'death." The poem presents an Ophelia figure, but one wedded to Christ's cruel treatment by man. The progress is murderous: the notion that madness is suffering (perhaps despairing of religious comfort) evolves into religion as madness. Christ's death, in the confines of this cinquain's logic, seems to have meant nothing, since death is an absolute victor. Thus, redemption and eternal life, foundational religious concepts, are significantly missing.

"The Warning" is equally frightening, almost Gothic, though closer to Emily Dickinson's voice, and offers a very Oriental image:

> Just now,
> Out of the strange
> Still dusk . . as strange, as still . .
> A white moth flew. Why am I grown
> So cold?

Again a question prevails, and there is a predominance of vowels, especially the "o" of a mute scream, the mouth, familiar, of one dead or dying, and the time at the end of day has alliteration to abet its insistent hush—"still," "strange," "still" yields more than one meaning, can imply doubt and hypnotic state. Yet, as usual, there is also the opposite reality, the contradictory force of motionless repetitions that project the cold stasis of death, a moth (white and destructive) out of its closet element, with the speaker leaving her own element (life) for death's strange shore. Dusk, moth, a chill, her imagined shiver and childlike query, the persona's awareness of the pattern, all combine into a felt awareness of self as a frail creature in a hostile environment. The fact that every word is monosyllabic, which compels a slow, deliberate reading, stresses an implacable design at work and adds to the sense of a dreaded mystery.

There are other cinquains in *Verse* which come close to this kind of brilliance but just miss. They miss, usually, because in them Crapsey tends to force her effects, becoming almost shrill, and violates the delicate internal balance of a form that has no room for excess, however slight or brief. "Anguish" (71) is a good example:

> Keep thou
> Thy tearless watch
> All night but when blue dawn
> Breathes on the silver moon, then weep!
> Then weep!

The repeated cry at poem's end, which simulates the emphatic stroke achieved at the conclusion of "The Guarded Wound" ("Too heavy!"), is far too melodramatic for a cinquain to support—besides spoiling the essential sprung-rhythm effect. As an experience, "Anguish" vibrates with emotion and cunning, the awareness that a tearless night watch demands release; but the need for crucial biographical information—the knowledge of Crapsey's own death watch each night—prevents it from approaching any enduring objective state of cathartic involvement for the reader; that is, it shuts out any purely textual comprehension (à la the New Criticism), which is always a flaw when not ameliorated by other factors, such as a surrealistic logos or a larger structural context.

Part of the problem undoubtedly stemmed from the fact that this particular cinquain seems to have been directly influenced by Revon's translation of a tonka by Satô Yoshikiyo:

> Tandi que je pense
> A des choses tristes, est-ce la lune
> Qui m'a dit: "Pleure!"
> Sur mon visage inquiet,
> Hélas! mes larmes![17]

From a Japanese standpoint, the moon itself was already traditionally identified with certain melancholy emotions, as Revon explained in a note, the moon *"s'associe par là même aux émotions tristes"* as *"les vieux souvenirs."*[18] But in English literature, the moon's rich symbolic values are much more complex and often contradictory in nature—J. Isaacs, the British critic, once observed that "it seems as though the history of poetry in all ages is the attempt to find new images for the moon"[19]—and thus demand that each poet establish his own frame of reference. Crapsey's poem has not done this sufficiently, despite its stark suggestiveness.

A more interesting near-miss is "Fate Defied" (76), which provides further confirmation of its author's penchant for adopting greyness as a symbol of defiance rather than dolor:

> As it
> Were tissue of silver
> I'll wear, O fate, thy gray,
> And go mistily radiant, clad
> Like the moon.

If nothing else, this certainly offers concrete proof that Crapsey regarded the cinquain as an accentual, not a syllabic, form, since the syllable count (2,6,6,9,3) bears no relation to the 2,4,6,8,2 arrangement usually associated with cinquain as a syllabic construct. The stresses, however, faithfully follow the 1,2,3,4,1 pattern found in the other cinquains, and Crapsey did include "Fate Defied" among the cinquains in *Verse*.

As a poem, "Fate Defied" fails at the elementary level of inadequate imagery, though the vowels help create a charming romantic atmosphere; and the accentual scheme takes no cognizance of secondary stresses, which not only destroys the required technical tightness but contributes somewhat to the flabbiness of the central metaphor. The problem is exacerbated by the dependence, again, upon moon as emblem, which will similarly weaken the more successful "Moon-shadows" (71), a cinquain that moves from moon-cast shadows on a motionless, windless night to "So still will be my heart when I/ Am dead." The simple climatic comparison between dead heart and moon shadows is effective, and yet its imagistic shorthand generates no widening echoes, no possibility of artistic transcendence.

Another cinquain that intrigues even as it defies its own internal logic—the logic of a hard surfaced, highly compressed objectification of experience—is "Release" (70), a personal metaphorical conceit for the brute physical pain that must have frequently driven the poet's mind into a near trance during her last months at the sanatorium:

> With swift
> Great sweep of her
> Magnificent arm my pain

>   Clanged back the doors that shut my soul
>   From life.

The idea assumes the daring, biographical intensity that characterized the best of Crapsey's late poetry, but as a cinquain it veers too
close to private opacity, to hermetic references for total success. Its
genuine accomplishment—that grand personification of an anguish
so fierce it engenders atheistic surrender to despair—paradoxically
damages its ability to spin a web of consequent metaphors.

A related failure haunts "Trapped" (71), where the poet's admirable attempt to reproduce a conversational idiom and style creates an
impressive, fatal aura of existence as day-to-day tedium, a slow form
of dying, although the ultimate poetic thrust falters:

>   Well and
>   If day on day
>   Follows, and weary year
>   On year . . . and ever days and years . .
>   Well?

Interestingly, by positing a vision of life absolutely without hope, the
cinquain seems to be prefiguring the *angst*-ridden void that would
later spur writers as different as Kafka and Beckett to turn back upon
language itself for survival. In fact, the deadly trail of days and years
so flatly unrolled in this unique poem, culminating in that damnable
and damning question, "Well?," is another striking instance of
Crapsey predicating her art upon a future aesthetic and condition,
however unconsciously. As a result, "Trapped" is more modern than
"Release" in its use of a personal wound for raw material and voice,
despite the latter's superior literary value.

Just how significant was Crapsey's debt to the Japanese for this
modernity can be estimated from the obvious echoes of Buson, a
master of the haiku, in "Trapped." As early as 1921, Royall Snow
pointed out its allegiance to a haiku by Buson, although he then made
the odd mistake of quoting an English translation of a haiku by Issa,
another master, in support of his assertion: "Granted this dewdrop
world is but/ A dewdrop world—this granted, yet. . ."[20] Professor
Smith has since cleared up the situation by demonstrating that the
relationship between "Trapped" and Buson came through Revon's
translation of the latter, which Crapsey had copied into her notes:
"Ah! le passé!/ Le temps où se sont accumulés/ Les jours lents!"[21] It is

easy to see how the mistake came about and how Crapsey was probably influenced by both haikus.

Two other cinquains from *Verse,* "Niagara" (77) and "Laurel in the Berkshires" (76), are travel poems, tourist reactions that do not quite surmount the innate limitations of their kind, though not nearly as offensive as the childishly exuberant "The Grand Canyon" (77), which begins with "By Zeus!" and goes downhill from there. Several respected critics have applauded "Niagara,"[22] but the technical mastery on display in the poem does not quite counter-balance its lack of depth:

> How frail
> Above the bulk
> Of crashing water hangs
> Autumnal, evanescent, wan,
> The moon.

Pictorially, "Niagara" is an integrated achievement, those three adjectives in the fourth line astutely, languidly building up to the soft owl-vowel expelling of breath a cinquain feeds on, and it is perhaps the closest Crapsey ever came to producing a true English haiku, which is no mean feat. Again, however, the dominant image, like the moon itself, hangs suspended in mid-air without hope of rescue from the charge of verbal misrepresentation. An imaginative critical mind could, of course, impose further dimensions, linking the moon to a familiar human sense of time's immutability, but the association would be forced under the circumstances, a case of unjustified symbol hunting.

In "Laurel in the Berkshires" the failure is more evident, though the poet's energetic mood of pagan celebration is infectious. The opening image, envisioning wood vegetation as "seafoam/ And coral," is a fine example of foreshadowing, preparing for the persona's peaking desire to "dream me mermaid in the sun's/ Gold flood." Unfortunately, the explosive quality of gleeful transformations conjures up a Romantic perspective that seems unearned, arbitrary, perhaps because the very briefness of the cinquain formula leaves little room for erecting complex cause-effect relationships. The elation, in other words, needs the amplification of a recognizable situation, which, ironically, might have been supplied by a mere change in title. The suggestion is not facetious, since a different title, however subtle, indicating a possible mood or problem scene might have given weight and direction to the poem's free-floating allusions.

Like "Release" before it, "Languor After Pain" (72) tries to isolate and preserve the reality of physical suffering, moving further ahead this time to that moment after pain has ebbed and "opiate weariness/ Settles on eye-lids, on relaxed/ Pale wrists." Also like "Release," the poem fails to project a necessary framework for metaphorical broadenings: the specific feeling, so specifically and beautifully conveyed, cries out for Eliot's "objective correlative," a concrete scene or object or reason to bear the burden of the vivid emotional state being delineated.

The cinquain entitled "Winter" (73) has the opposite problem of laboring to wrench a universal, seasonal reality back closer to home, toward a specific eye:

> The cold
> With steely clutch
> Grips all the land . . alack,
> The little people in the hills
> Will die!

Even keeping in mind that the reference to the "little people" is both a cute Dickinsonism and a legitimate appeal to a distant ballad-pastoral tradition, the lead from a vibrant, severe winter setting to what it portends in an historical sense flounders not on the rocks of a too personal expression, but on the softer shoals of what might be termed artificial animism. Though undoubtedly sincere in its concern for nature's cruel blow against its "lesser" creatures, including the poet herself, "Winter" does not quite convince of its seriousness, hovering too close to a saccharin whimsy for conviction. Its shallowness is highlighted when juxtaposed with the more moving "Shadow" (75):

> A-sway
> On red rose,
> A golden butterfly . .
> And on my heart a butterfly
> Night-wing'd.

The elements here are traditional—for example, "red rose" and "golden butterfly," which is not inappropriate in a form based upon Japanese lyric modes—but the summary metaphor of the black-winged butterfly on her heart transforms them into something else, something more, a unique conjunction of vision and feeling. Whatever the precise significance of the climatic metaphor—fear, uncertainty, the stain and strain of human mortality—it almost saves the poem from itself. The shadow of death carries a religious connotation as well, if only in terms of a somewhat removed biblical allusion, but the cinquain remains bleakly secular, unrelieved by hope.

In "Refuge in Darkness" (77-78), the sole solution to the shadow and sorrow—the approach of oblivion—seems to lie with an embracing of the shadow's mother, night, night as a dim blue veil which the speaker wants to use as a blindfold against her own painful insights: "I will bind close my eyes that are/ So weary." But, again, the experience is too limited for complete poetic efficency, though it is easy to empathize with the general mood. Roses—perennial fodder for all poets and Crapsey in particular—are returned to in an untitled cinquain that had for its epigram, "He's killed the may and he's laid her by/ To bear the red rose company" (74). In Crapsey's poem the "may" becomes a white rose for a reaffirmation of strict duality in nature and art, with the speaker accepting the white rose's "Ensanguined sister" for her heart's companion, her heart's "Shed blood." *Blood to blood* appears to be the relationship sought, ritualized, perhaps a belief that the purity (and its Christian sanction in piety) Crapsey had celebrated in so many of her earlier poems was now deemed inadequate, and that she would rather choose life itself, despite the heavy price paid in wounds and unsated passions. Anguish is thus formalized, and once again manifested as polar verities in a severe Manichean cosmos.

About the rest of the cinquains in *Verse*, nine in all, not too much need be said, except to note that their failures are practically absolute. All of them are consequences of clearly derivative experiences, are either commentaries upon literary materials, as in "Susanna and the Elders" (72), "Saying of Il Haboul" (75-76), "The Death of Holofernes" (76), and "Now Barabas Was a Robber" (77), or travel pieces, such as "Arbutus" (73-74), "Roma Aeterna" (74), and "The Grand Canyon," already cited. Two of them, "Snow" (71) and "Youth" (72), attempt originality; and "Snow" at least projects the excitement of a child's enthusiasm to help hide its lack of depth:

> Look up . . .
> From bleakening hills

> Blows down the light, first breath
> Of wintry wind . . . look up, and scent
> The snow![23]

But in "Youth" the young persona mouths a cliché, which spoils the cinquain's supposedly ironic intent, denying that old age and death are possible in his world, "the strange/ And ignominious end of old/ Dead folk!" Crapsey's own shortened life makes this idea seem more startling that it is, blurring its prosaic wit somewhat.

The seven other cinquains are guilty of the same kind of goodnatured, adolescent cleverness, including "Roma Aeterna," which Winters expressed a liking for, finding it "similar" to "Snow," but concluding that "the subject is more impressive and the poem has more power."[24] Its coy address to "Romulus" and sticky-sweet climax—the birds on his "olden Palatine" are perceived as still singing—do not bear him out, however, and make brittle the very sheen of condensed lyric beauty the poet was struggling to proclaim.

A more worthy failure is "Susanna and the Elders," which produces the restraint necessary for genuine irony:

> "Why do
> You thus devise
> Evil against her?" "For that
> She is beautiful, delicate:
> Therefore."

Its failure, an honorable one, stems essentially from the psychological thinness of the material itself, not from its technique. On the positive side, the use of a dialogue form to carry the irony and the brilliant placement of "Therefore" evoke an ambiance of understated mockery that is in perfect keeping with the poem's cynical look back at a "simpler" biblical world.

III   Miscellaneous Cinquains

Of the seven cinquains found among Crapsey's papers which she had presumably chosen not to include in *Verse* despite their finished states, only three achieve any degree of poetic success: "To an Unfaithful Lover" (102), "Blue Hyacinths" (103), and an untitled translation (104) from Michel Revon's version of a tonka by Satô Yoshikiyo. In "To an Unfaithful Lover," a synthetic awkwardness tends to mar a valid, if romantic, complaint against a casual rake, echoing some of the poet's Vassar poems:

> What words
> Are left thee then
> Who has squandered on thy
> Forgetfulness eternity's
> *I love?*

Like several similar poems about love, including perhaps "The Guarded Wound,"[25] there is an underlying bitterness present that, at least biographically, suggests loss. As artifice, "To an Unfaithful Lover" proceeds smoothly enough, with the assistance of unobtrusive alliterations, until that fatal fourth line, where the notion is lucid but the choice of words and their arrangement downright unfortunate, too clumsy and too abstract for a lyric line to support. It ruins the icily witty play upon the lover's endless and endlessly false avowals of love.

This force of wit can also be found in the more orthodox "Blue Hyacinths," a cinquain that imaginatively weds the flowers to the ancient world so often evoked by the Romantics, their beautiful scent envisioned as "perfumed immortal breath sighing/ Of Greece." The poem emits a positive, dreamy quality that summons up deliberate echoes of Keats, Shelley, and Bryon, while also emulating a haiku instant in time: capturing a fleeting image from nature and causing it to vibrate with hidden, fecund meanings.

The untitled translation from Revon's French is more ordinary in aim and realization:

> Why have
> I thought the dew
> Ephemeral when I
> Shall rest so short a time, myself,
> On earth?

Wisely, Crapsey had not sought too literal an equivalent for Revon—whose translation commences with "*Comment ai-je pu penser/ Que la rosee*"—substituting "dew" for the wornout rose image, thereby transforming "rest" into a completely appropriate verb. If unoriginal, not only as translation but as a poem, the nexus between dew and human mortality has more power than would have been possible with another tedious rose allusion. Also, the isolation of "myself" inside commas forces the cinquain to hesitate in such a way as to emphasize the sharp contrast between final individual existence and solid, massive earth.

The other four cinquains, "To a Hermit Thrush" (102-03), "The Source" (103), "For Lucas Cranach's Eve" (103), and another untitled one (104), have little to recommend them. Still, "The Source" hints at a mystery behind human character:

> Thou hast
> Drawn laughter from
> A well of secret tears
> And thence so elvish it rings,—mocking
> And sweet.

Who or what weighs down "The Source" is unknown, but the odd combination of "elvish" and "secret tears" intimates potential profundity, if too "sweet" in the end for much real substance.

The untitled cinquain—concerned with "the first faint breath/ Of snow" and probably a companion to the cinquain entitled "Snow"—is simply another superficial pastoral exercise that possesses neither new insights nor original imagery. Crapsey insists upon reiterating that, like remorseless winter, nature itself exists without recourse, monstrous and distinct from human life or influence. The artist understands this, and "To a Hermit Thrush" utilizes a reference to Tristram in an effort to translate the bird's song into a symbol for the artist's perpetual sorrow:

> Art thou
> Not kin to him
> Who loved Mark's wife and both
> Died for it? O, thou harper in
> Green woods?

The mythical allusion adds a measure of density, but the final cliché destroys much of its ironic impact.

And yet, Crapsey's many failures in the cinquain form only serve, in the end, to underline the genuine excellence of those that did succeed. When considering the latter, including the important handful of "near-misses," it is obvious that the invention of the cinquain was one certain way for the poet finally to express her obsession with death in a fashion that suited her preference for technical restraint, extreme compression. Along the way, besides striving to introduce Japanese forms into English and creating a viable approach to Imagism, Crapsey added a significant number of delightful lyrics to the store of American poetry.

CHAPTER 6

Other Late Poems

B^Y and large, those critics aware of Adelaide Crapsey, including
Edmund Wilson,[1] have tended to value her almost solely on the
basis of the cinquains, ignoring or disparaging her other later verses.
This emphasis, I believe, has resulted in the loss of several valuable
poems from our literary consciousness, poems such as "Song," "To
the Dead in the Grave-Yard Under My Window," "My Birds That
Fly No Longer," and "Lines Addressed to My Left Lung," which are
unique in their refreshing candor, directness, and almost experimental approach to conversational ease. In many ways, these verses
prefigure the personal lyric style that surfaced soon after Crapsey's
death in the poetry of Edna St. Vincent Millay, Sara Teasdale, Elinor
Wylie, and, to a lesser degree, Louise Bogan, while also paralleling
the Imagist revolution being carried forward by the indefatigable
Amy Lowell, at least in terms of concentrating upon an avoidance of
traditional rhetoric and Georgian excess.

Their thematic focus upon an obsession with death and their refusal
to entertain notions of religious salvation, of metaphysical escape
clauses, also gave them a distinct secular cast, a pioneer attitude that
anticipated a much later ethos in American poetry. A few of
them—specifically "Lines Addressed to My Left Lung" and "To the
Dead in the Grave-Yard Under My Window"—projected conversational narratives that seem to make them a branch of the modernist
stream that had its source in Whitman (and perhaps Dickinson),
mirroring the nativist or populist currents at work in Lindsay and
Sandberg and emptying, eventually, into the broader genius of
William Carlos Williams and his aesthetic of "no ideas but in things."

I *Poems in* Verse

Of the later poems besides the cinquains which Crapsey intended
for inclusion in *Verse*, "Song" (87) is the most impressive, perhaps the

finest she ever wrote—an opinion shared by Gregory and Zaturenska.[2] According to Mary Osborn, "Song" emerged in the spring of 1912 as a purely metrical exercise, the poet reciting "the vowel sounds alone to show the sequence of rising and falling tones" to a friend,[3] and the poem itself seems to be deliberate variation on the French triolet form. But it is the felicitous merger of form and content in "Song" which makes it such a moving, eerily potent performance. The fairytale aura—darkened by a subtle menace, as are all effective fairy tales—provides a perfect vehicle for conveying Crapsey's repressed despair and obsession: "I make my shroud but no one knows,/So shimmering fine it is and fair." This reminds one of Millay's "The Harp Weaver" and Landor's untitled lyric that begins, "Mother, I cannot mind my wheel", in its insistence upon a child's plaintive voice and vision and its central image. The assonance maintains its light melody with a soft deceptiveness—learned from Milton's "Lycidas"[4]—which helps emphasize the harsh dichotomy between lyric form and bleak message, summing up the poet's own last years in the process:

> In door-way where the lilac blows,
> Humming a little wandering air,
> I make my shroud and no one knows
> So shimmering fine it is and fair.

But the thrust is not hermetic, not flawed by a lack of relevant information, because the brief poem manages to encapsulate the artist as a generic figure, heroic and pathetic, both a child and a sort of Everywoman gifted by a talent which must also encompass a constant awareness of death's steady advance. Beauty, in fact, is seen as being weaved from the very fabric of human mortality. More to the point, as the probably unconscious or accidental echo of Whitman's famous Lincoln elegy tends to reinforce, "Song" is a dirge for self—a Romantic motif—the penultimate irony of art extinguishing personality, though hardly in the fashion celebrated by Eliot's "Tradition and the Individual Talent." Also, the lightness of tone and the triolet's interlocking rhymes and refrains evoke an ancient ballad world where tragedy is always song's truest note.

It is hardly surprising to discover that none of the other late poems in *Verse* quite measure up to "Song" in their total effects, although "The Lonely Death" (96), another poignant manifestation of an autumnal self, comes very close. The speaker—a probable offspring of Dickinson's persona—is imagined preparing her own funeral, and the ritual has an iambic balance and ease to it that is cunningly smooth, deceptively so, music once again lulling the mind away from the flesh's morbid message. Using her own daily awareness of icy dawns at Lake Saranac, Crapsey returns to the familiar emblem of a "gray" sunrise that incorporates "waters of ice," loneliness, and a funeral rite that could be mocking poetry's formalities: "myself/ Will shiver, and shrive myself,/ Alone in the dawn, and anoint/ Forehead and feet and hands."

The touching climax of "The Lonely Death"—"Will lay myself straight in my bed/ And draw the sheet under my chin"—has the necessary air of terrible inevitability which is made more moving by the intimation of a child going quietly to bed; but the poem's strict adherence to a regular meter casts a slight pall of mannered artifice over the whole, defeating its own purpose, ruining the mood just enough to prevent maximum impact. Though nearly as effective as "Song," betraying the same concern for contrasting secret death with external order, "The Lonely Death" is a bit too strained for complete involvement, emotion blunted by technical prissiness.

All the other late poems intended for inclusion in *Verse,* which are as obsessed as "Song," "The Lonely Death," and so many of the cinquains with the theme of treacherous mortality, are less successful in matching style to meaning. Six of them, however, must be viewed as close calls, strong, interesting, often skillful misses that are usually marred by a single fatal flaw: "Mad-Song" (92-93), "The Witch" (93-94), "Angélique" (90-91), "Night" (89), "Dirge" (81), and "Warning to the Mighty" (80).

"Mad-Song," for instance, is fitfully fascinating in its acute depiction of the madness behind sanity that must threaten any sensitive soul confronting unavoidable dissolution. The primary personification of griefs as "Grey goalers" is not too Georgian, and the governing metaphor of a human being imprisoned by her own sorrow is well-organized—and familiar to Crapsey readers. Furthermore, the sense again of a hidden anguish, a Kirkegaardian "sickness unto death" that death alone—"The refuge of black gates"—can relieve, appears valid within the closed context of the poem. But the fatal flaw in this case stems from the attempt to stretch out what is essentially a very narrow, if thus intense, perception. Fewer stanzas might have made a crucial difference.

In "Angélique," a more powerful poem, the flaw is the less intrusive one of another rigid, unimaginative rhyme scheme—the trimetric lines, though slow-footed, are too frail to bear its weight. But the poem has a somber narrative quality that is enticing and uses its mythical figure to good effect, a white-robed Antigone bearing the Statue of Liberty's "flickering light" in her endless quest:

> Have you seen Angélique . .
> At night I hear her moan,
> And I shiver in my bed;
> She wanders all alone,
> She cannot find the dead.

"Dirge," on the other hand, reverts too readily to the high Romantic tone and language Crapsey had been apt to imitate in her ornate, otiose college pieces—"Never again the lark/Thou wilt hear"—although the image of dusk tapping "at thy window-sill" is charming in the best sense. Only the title and a knowledge of the poet's biography, however, add poignancy to the axis concept of lost songs, or lost opportunities: "Though ever love call and call/ Thou wilt not hear at all, / My dear, my dear." But in "The Sun-Dial," which could very well have been an embryonic cinquain that never came to term, the simple repetitions achieve a persuasive Gothic atmosphere, implying fertile, dreaded, unseen Poe-like depths:

> Every day,
> Every day,
> Tell the hours
> By their shadows,
> By their shadows.

Though longer and more elaborate, "Night" attains a similar measure of dark intensity with far subtler materials, moving from nature's day miracle of crickets singing in the noon sun through twilight winds among "slim marsh/grasses" to the night climax at "a lily pond," where it is the waters that "sway" moonlit leaves and "curled long stems." The single-line refrain of "And I cannot sleep" acts as a potent comment upon the daily sequence—ticked off with metronomic regularity and precision—of natural events being articulated, a sequence that reflects, in miniature, the much vaster cosmic processes that always have as their terminus a death, an implacable ending. Rebirth, along with any other idea of a religious counterforce, is once more notable by its absence, as it is in most of the cinquains and other late poems. However personally committed to a Christian universe—her letters make clear her dependence upon her Bible—Crapsey as artist remained secular, pragmatic, Darwinian, which is perhaps why her best work gleams with such a modernistic shine.

Just how secular is evident in "Warning to the Mighty," which is almost cynically bitter, if not blatantly antiChristian, in its mocking warning:

> Ere the hornèd owl hoot
> Once and twice and thrice there shall
> Go among the blind brown worms
> News of thy great burial;
> When the pomp is passed away,
> "Here's a King," the worms will say.

Christ's warning to a rich man is a possible echo, but the clear reference to Peter hearing the cock crow at his betrayal would imply—in a delicious switch of meaning—that Christ himself was not immune to the worms. A youthful reading of Poe's "The Conqueror Worm" might stand behind this poem as well, and the image of "blind brown worms"—so effective in a Gothic manner—spotlights the existence of blind forces at work in the universe that exhibit no awareness of human values, human egos.

This secular cynicism gains a social dimension in "The Witch," which appeared in the *Century Magazine* a few months after its author's death. In the witch projection, Crapsey assumes the voice of Woman through history, particularly those individuals who had dared to assert themselves, had dared to utilize their brains and skills and even sex appeal in a quest for power and art: "My lover, he who dreamed the Sphinx,/ Learned all his dreaming from my eyes." Greece and Italy, twin symbols of the Old World's highest civilizations, knew her well, though her roles were limited by a male chauvinistic society to either "Madonna to a painter-lad" or "mistress to a Medici."

The Christian theocracy of the New World also could not abide the rebellion this woman represented and "burnt her on the Salem green," which provides a tidy allegory for the antifeminine bias Crapsey must have detected and deplored in her religion, inheriting her father's own liberal skepticism regarding the matter of organized rituals and handed-down myths. "The Witch" is an intriguing poem, not so much for its antiChristian flavor, which was certainly not unusual in the late poetry, as for its rare effort to mate this element with a feminist, humanist perspective. Rarer still, the poem is *not* death-obsessed, at least not with death as a personal, primal motivation for art. Poetically, "The Witch" is both clever and smoothly manipulated, attesting to Crapsey's professional maturity and sureness.

Two other late poems that were to appear in *Verse*, "Chimes" (91-92) and "The Mourner" (88-89), are distinct failures, dragged to earth by unconvincing poetic devices and a penchant for earlier stylistic excesses. In "The Mourner" the attempt is earnest, a cliché solemnly intoned by the last line, "For the forgotten dead are dead indeed," and the central figure is, occasionally, skillfully persuasive in her handling of language and image: "Where cypresses, more black than night is black, / Border straight paths, or where, on hillside slopes, / The dim grey glimmer of the olive trees / Lies like a breath, a ghost, upon the dark." But frequent lapses into rhetoric, too many stabs at preRaphaelite flourishes—as in "the veiled stars withdraw / Their tremulous light"—ruin the poem's progression, and produce lush stage directions rather than vital poetry.

Lacking a direct personal focus, "The Mourner" simply fails to convey its ultimate seriousness, despite a sincere purpose. It is too much the moral lesson; a felt experience never emerges from behind its Romantic mask. In a similar fashion, "Chimes" reads like a standard exercise in exclamatory versification, guilty, I think, of an adolescent adherence to Poe's worst side from beginning to end:

> The rose new-opening saith
> And the dew of the morning saith,
> (Fallen leaves and vanished dew)
> Remember death.

> *Ding dong bell*
> *Ding dong bell*

Such self-conscious strivings for dramatic effect first blunt, then negate entirely the genuine desperation which must have been feeding the poem's heart: "May-moon thin and young / In the sky, / Ere you wax and wane / I shall die"—the strongest lines in the poem, although they depend upon a hackneyed personification and another appeal to biographical data for emotional resonance. Even an old nemesis, Death itself, Death as Lover in this instance, utters his caressing threat with creaky ballad stiffness: "Thy gold hair likes me well / And thy blue eyes." It all sounds reminiscent of the lurid,

1890s technique and milieu manifested in "Evil," "Pierrot," "La Morte," and other works from Crapsey's London period. If the last stanza does manage a slight recovery in metaphors of roses as candle flames and lilies like funeral bells, it still cannot completely escape the ineptitude of an artifice devoid of original ideas. Worse, the *"Ding dong bell"* refrains either amuse or bore rather than disturb or haunt.

These two embarrassing failures point up the relative poverty of Crapsey's image making facilities, a constant problem. With devastating clarity, they expose her heavy reliance upon inherited symbols and a handful of sharp personal observations for her main figures of speech, e.g., roses, dew, grey, dawns and dusks, allegorical suns, emblematic moons, deadly winter settings. They also stress, however, how amazing the successes remain, erected as they were on such narrow foundations.

II *Foreshadowings*

Crapsey wrote three poems late in her short life which she decided, perhaps out of shyness, not to include in *Verse*, but which deserve special consideration: "Lines Addressed to My Left Lung Inconveniently Enamoured of Plant-Life" (119), "To the Dead in the Grave-Yard Under My Window" (101-02), and "My Birds That Fly No Longer" (105). Their titles alone, so uncharacteristic in length and directness, jar the eye. The first, one of the few poems which can be precisely dated, having been written in February, 1914 at the sanatorium and sent home in a letter,[5] grew out of a medical examination which had confirmed the dangerous condition of Crapsey's lung.

The tart, morbid wit that informs and orders the poem is much like the "black humor" of the later 1950s, and perhaps for the same reason: humor is often the only sane response to maddening, absolute despair, as evidenced in the "gallows humor" that flourished in the concentration camps of World War II. Thus, the invasion of deadly tuberculosis germs is reduced to "Plant-Life" in love with Crapsey's left lung, and part of the "fun" (mask or not) of the poem resides in the very artificiality of the mental gymnastics behind such transferences, self-conscious in the manner of a stage farce. The initial stanza firmly establishes the scene and the bitter-sweet tone it seems to evoke:

> It was, my lung, most strange of you,
> A freak I cannot pardon,

> Thus to transform yourself into
> A vegetable garden.

Even the heavy meter and jangling rhyme scheme conspire to increase the humor, tipping the reader's emotions offbalance to the point where the terrible situation seems almost nullified, defused. But, like any other form of artistic understatement, the black humor does eventually tend to intensify what is being underplayed. The frightening discovery and tragedy of tuberculosis, as if the body had been betrayed by a Fifth Column, becomes an excrescent horror, and the last stanza of the three contrasts a more normal reaction to the illness—"lament" and "crazy"—with the humorous concept of the afflicted lung's own self-deception: "For all I know, serene, content, / You think yourself a daisy!" Though scarcely a major poem, and not so intended by any means, "Lines Addressed to My Left Lung" is effective throughout, a relaxed, flawless capture of a comic mode and voice not frequently pursued by Crapsey's poetry. Its general ease and wit are modern in their pert refusal of tragic hyperbole.

"My Birds That Fly No Longer" is a different matter, much more typical of Crapsey's other late poems in its attempt to articulate a symbolic statement about the remorseless approach of death. This brief lyric, which consists of two quatrains, is strongly reminiscent of Francis Thompson in language and sound, and in its fundamental subject matter, a loss of faith. Victorian "high seriousness" prevails.

Tightly structured, the first stanza is a question addressed to a flock of birds, asking if they had forgotten how "near the heavens lie?" Heaven and sky are yoked together through a cloud image, "Drooping, sick-pinion'd," which sets up the poem's basic construct, its parallel lines of touchstone (literal scene) and metaphor. The second stanza shifts from birds to self and takes on a broader allegorical value:

> The air that once I knew
> Whispered celestial things;
> I weep who hear no more
> Upward and rushing wings.

Suddenly, associated with the earlier coupling of sky and heaven, the birds have been metamorphosed into something greater, possibly into angels—an interpretation which can be justified by "celestial things" as well. The speaker's anguish, then, has been transmuted into a definite spiritual dilemma, arising, apparently, from her inability to accept the miracles of religious belief; that is, to accept a universe rife with mystery, supernatural potentialities, now that actual death looms near. It confirms the patent lack of Christian conviction evident in the best of the cinquains and a number of other late poems, including "To the Dead in the Grave-Yard Under My Window."

The latter, which Crapsey dated "November, 1913," emerged from a very real and very disturbing situation at the sanatorium: her window faced a cemetery, where she occasionally had to witness a funeral's last stages, reminding her graphically of the fate lurking at her own bedside.

Osborn deemed "To the Dead in the Grave-Yard Under My Window" an incomplete experience, "the material out of which great poems are made, but it is not a great poem,"[6] and Professor Smith claims that the "poem's greatest interest is for the biographer."[7] But I have to disagree, feeling the poem is far more successful than either critic would concede. It is a powerful recreation of an interior monologue in the Browning style that takes full advantage of dramatic, modernistic "plain speech" to proclaim a universal condition: man's mortal terror when religious immortality is no longer a feasible illusion. Propelled, energized, encouraged by a voice too furious for normal restraints—the subtitle, "Written in A Moment Of Exasperation," is an apology from a proper young lady, not a poet—Crapsey's line is freer, longer, almost Whitmanesque from start to finish, determinately conversational. It is also, inevitably, closer to prose, commencing with the persona's irked questioning of the distant (yet not distant enough) corpses: "How can you lie so still?"

The dramatic mode has thus been established from the beginning, and abets the poem's dominant conceit, the living link being forged between the doomed girl in Trudeau's Sanatorium and the dead people in the graveyard haunting her days and nights. The persona keenly resents what she imagines to be the passive stillness of the dead, regretting that "not one ghost comes forth/ To take its freedom of the midnight hour," and this notion need not be stretched too far to incorporate an obvious unhappiness with a lost faith, a lost innocence. The invidious yet puerile images of the buried corpses—"pallid mouldering acquiescent folk"—are loose but distinct, deliberately harsh and extreme, evolving into an ironic commentary upon useless, irritating medical advice, "Lie still/ And rest; be patient," which the poet treats as a "text" straight from those "row on row" of "Meek habitants of unresented graves."

Contrasted to them, and to the persona's bleak situation, is the splendid array of nature visible beyond them both, "purple wood-lands" and "blue mountains," which the persona would love to plunder, but which only her eyes "may follow." Rebellion is the crucial motif, a brave and angry refusal to accept death, her doctor's orders, and the lesson of submission preached by "the many sayings of the wise"—the lesson of Christ ("Sermon on the Mount") and Christianity. The persona's wisdom, earned under fire in the constant battle with death, stems from the realization that resignation is "sister to defeat," that she must keep "the edge of deprivation sharp." Her toughminded defiance of fate and man, "I'll not be patient. I will not lie still," follows the advice Dylan Thomas would proffer his dying father many decades later in "Do Not Go Gentle into That Good Night."

But at the end, a grim reality holds sway as the "despot of our days and lord of dust" quenches all Romantic rebellion: *"Yes; yes . . . Wilful and petulant but now / As dead and quiet as the others are."* Escape is impossible, foolish, and the ultimate wisdom does indeed become, ironically, what had been denied so vehemently earlier, the flesh truth "each body and ghost of you hath heard/ That in your graves do therefore lie so still." Undoubtedly, "To the Dead in the Grave-Yard Under My Window" could be shorter, tighter, less self-indulgent, but its harrowing illumination of a secular, death-haunted world, which some of Millay's finest sonnets would also encompass, achieves the intensity of genuine drama. The technique of having the persona address the dead creates a theatrical vehicle for what is a spiritual dilemma, while the relaxed, casual language adds a diary-like aura of engrossing immediacy.

These three poems seem to go against the grain of Crapsey's entire life and career, to violate the aesthetic of restraint—technical and emotional—which had shaped the mask she used most often to keep the world at bay and to preserve her sanity under the relentless threat of a terminal illness. They embody a fierce *cri de couer* that had been denied for too long, and, as such, burst free of her usual, sometimes excessive commitment to the problems of technique. Not that they lack formal engineering. Quite the contrary. All three evince regular meters and/or rhyme schemes and never hesitate to make good use of numerous other "tricks of the trade," for example, assonance and alliteration. But the uncharacteristic expansiveness of the line, especially in "Lines Addressed to My Left Lung" and "To the Dead in the Grave-Yard Under My Window," foreshadows the eventual movement of one American current through Imagism and into the relaxed diction of William Carlos Williams and such disciples of his as David Ignatow.

As a result, these three poems can be read today as if written by a contemporary, a contemporary keenly conscious of our age's godless desolation and seeming need for confessional relief. Though Crapsey refused to make them part of her first collection, which she knew was her last as well, the reason was probably personal rather than aesthetic. They are simply too naked, venting negative emotions— the natural sense of futility and rage inspired by her illness—that her upbringing could not concede existed, at least in herself. Her great love of privacy and decorum, along with her public allegiance to Christian principles and teachings, would have been compromised by such unvarnished assaults upon the inner self.

And yet, she did write and preserve them, and their unconventionality bestows a modernity and power not frequently found in her less daring endeavors. Nor were the attitudes they expressed divorced from the personality that nurtured them. Like her father, Crapsey was a rebel at heart, though less inclined to exhibit it in public. Indeed, when her friend Elsie Draper read "To the Dead in the Grave-Yard Under My Window," she found it "quite characteristic of Adelaide Crapsey," after supplying a sketch of the poet that seems true to the profoundly divided nature of her life and art: "I knew Adelaide as a very adventurous person; almost a rebel; who was also, strangely enough, a person of such diffidence as nearly to counteract the vigor of her personality."[8]

III   *Miscellaneous Later Poems*

There are a small handful of other late poems not included in *Verse* which, unlike the three just discussed, deserve their neglect. The best of them, "Old Love" (105) and "As I Went" (114-15), are strung between the poles of love and death, possessing a certain melodic grace and brevity that is not unpleasant, if far from major. "Old Love" in particular attains a rather high level of rueful, lyric intensity:

> More dim than waning moon
> Thy face, more faint

> Than is the falling wind
> Thy voice, yet do
> Thine eyes most strangely glow,
> Thou ghost . . thou ghost.

The images are familiar, unoriginal, but used to good purpose for the most part, aided by vowel-soft echoes of a "falling wind" that suggest more than simple regret. Moon as face, wind as voice, and the glow in the distance like the apparitional features of a person once beloved swoop down close to some ancient, human primacy of emotion that is almost archetypal.

However, the Oriental delicacy of "Old Love" flattens out a bit when attached to an allegory of death in "As I Went," where Crapsey is apparently intent upon reproducing another "modern" version of some traditional ballad or another. Influenced by Thompson again, the poem uses four refrain-like stanzas to progress from death as hound through death as bird and as fish to the climactic personification of Death entering her own home and last refuge:

> As I went, as I went
>   In my house, in my house,
> I heard, I heard,
>   A footfall, a footfall
>   Closely behind me—
> Death . . it is death . .

The repetitions certainly have a rapid, hypnotic effect, but once more the imagery and governing concept lack the excitement of original metaphor. The stark simplicity of the structure is not at fault, since it does simulate a neurotic obsessiveness and draws the reader into its neomedieval realm, and the bleak subject matter varies little from that explored by so many of the successful cinquains. Nor is the theme slight. In fact, it is a bold variation upon Crapsey's frequent thrusts against basic Christian doctrine in her last phase: unlike Thompson, it is not God who is stalking her, but secular, absolute death—oblivion, not metaphysical meaning—making "As I Went" a possible parody, albeit a bitter one, of "The Hound of Heaven."

Whatever their limitations, "Old Love" and "As I Went" present a professional front at every turn and reveal a cool craftsman at work, which cannot be said about two other poems from this group, "The Event" (106) and "Tears" (109). The former returns to Crapsey's earlier—perhaps these *are* earlier—weakness for Keatsian manipula-

tions of classical myths and themes. In this instance, it is the three
Fates who are envisioned as bent over their knitting, the fabric of
human destiny. "Lo" has also been revived, along with an adolescent
urge toward rhetorical excess, as the final two lines demonstrate:

> Weave, Fates! And what your spinstry weaves I'll
>   forthwith wear
> And if it clothe me for the day or death's no air.

Though courageous in light of the poet's biography, such shrill
sentiments do not a poem make. Further, the clumsiness of the
language, which contrasts sharply with the lyrical deftness shown in
"Old Love" and "As I Went," indicated that Crapsey herself was not
paying very much attention when she wrote the poem. What is
interesting from the psychological standpoint is the subtle connection
suggested between spinsterhood and death.

In "Tears" there is a similar sense of poetic retrogression, as
rhetoric prevails over a more characteristic sparseness. Any modern
poem which commences with "The immemorial grief of all years/
Burdens my heart sorely" is obviously doomed to archaic precon-
sciousness. At the core of "Tears" a dialogue between soul and self is
supposed to pulse—as Yeats might have understood its dynamics—
but the diction employed prevents dramatic interactions, becomes a
kind of self-parody, while the absence of images tends to imitate the
prose of a murky sermon. At poem's end, the voice of the soul offers
nothing more fruitful than a truism blurred by clouds of sterile
oratory:

> Never and never shalt thou be
> As I. Weep; for weeping and hard pain
> Of loss measure joy of last visioned gain.

Neither philosopher nor theologian, despite a fascination with the
latter, Crapsey had made the mistake of emulating the jargon of both
at their worst.

It is easy to see that the late poems only achieve maturity when
shackled to the extreme restraints of style and form forged from a
careful consideration of Oriental methods. Still, the three exceptions
discussed in the previous section also imply that Crapsey could very
well have been on the brink—with the aid of Browning and her own
honesty—of moving with adept sureness into a newer, plainer, less
Imagistic mode when death intervened.

CHAPTER 7

"A Poetry of Personal Identity"

ADELAIDE Crapsey's position in the pantheon of American literature has never been clear. Like most authors, her reputation tended to suffer a severe decline once the dramatic impact of her early death had worn off, despite the continued, relative success of *Verse*, which went through six editions between 1915 and 1938, and the persistent inclusion of certain cinquains and a few other late poems in several respected anthologies. During the years immediately following her death, critics and reviewers were fairly unanimous in their praise, reflecting, perhaps, the then-current excitement generated by Amy Lowell's crusade on behalf of Imagism and her own poetry.[1] Alfred Kreymborg, self-proclaimed spokesman for the "New Verse" of Stevens, Sandberg, Aiken, *et al.*, printed thirteen of Crapsey's cinquains in a 1916 edition of his *Others* magazine.[2]

The magazine and newspaper reviews of *Verse* were naturally deficient with regard to specific comment, but seemed united, if a bit uncomfortable at times, in their appreciation of Crapsey's gift for compression and Imagistic control. An anonymous reviewer (with the initials F. H.) in the *New Republic* quoted from several cinquains "to illustrate Miss Crapsey's greatest gift, a decorative one," while also insisting that amid "the heightened and narrowed intensity of these impressions one may detect pathology," which hinted at the darker undercurrents stirred up the secular, bitter obsession with death that filled *Verse*.[3]

This uneasiness found concrete expression in the Baltimore *Post Express* review as well, where the reviewer tried to balance aesthetic and human considerations: "The poems are strikingly original, although some of them have more psychological than literary value."[4] At the furthest edge of sentimental absurdity, various other notices emphasized the positive aspects of Crapsey's achievement to the point of sublime tears, more influenced by the life than its literature, as in the Detroit *Times*, where the unknown reviewer was overcome enough to concede that "It is impossible to put into words what we feel about these poems."[5] Only Alice Corbin Henderson's review in *Poetry* (Chicago) admitted that it was "hard to separate Adelaide Crapsey's poems from the circumstances of her death."[6]

But the Boston *Transcript* review—one of the more erudite and intelligent—observed that *Verse* fell within "the scope of the modern movement for new and concentrated forms," and singled out several cinquains and "To the Dead in the Grave-Yard Under My Window" for special admiration.[7] Perhaps the single most enthusiastic review was that in the *New Republic* by Llewellyn Jones, who celebrated *Verse* as "a book of poetry that will live."[8] His prediction, however, was not quite realized in the decades after 1916, although Llewellyn himself, Harriet Monroe, and Marsden Hartley hailed Crapsey's art in subsequent collections of their essays,[9] and as late as 1928 the British poet and critic, J. C. Squire, wrote in the London *Observer*—while reviewing *The Oxford Book of American Verse*—that after Emily Dickinson "incomparably the finest woman-poet America has produced was Adelaide Crapsey."[10]

These affirmative voices were drowned out, however, as Imagism gave way before the full force of the larger American poetic renaissance initiated by Pound and Eliot, a renaissance so rich in diverse talent that it produced one major figure after another, including Stevens, Frost, Aiken, and Williams—all contemporaries or near contemporaries of Crapsey who lived (and developed) far beyond her. For all intents and purposes, again with the exception of a handful of cinquains and other late verses, Crapsey's poetry and most serious criticism of it disappeared from the literary scene during the turbulent years from the 1920s to the present.[11] And yet there were always one or two astute commentators, usually poets themselves, willing to champion Crapsey's slender *oeuvre*.

In their intelligent, usually perceptive *A History of American Poetry* (1942), for instance, Horace Gregory and Marya Zaturenska devoted seven pages to Crapsey, characterizing her as "as fine a minor talent as has ever appeared in American poetry,"[12] and Louis Untermeyer was an early supporter, printing a selection of her verse in his influential anthology, *Modern American Poetry*, which first appeared in 1919.[13] He also wrote warmly about her work in *The New Era in American Poetry* (1919), essentially a collection of essays and reviews, in which he rightly noted the link to Dickinson and saluted Crapsey's "sincerity of emotion and perfection of craft that proclaims the genius."[14] Another early supporter was Alfred Kreymborg.

Besides printing her cinquains in *Others*, he extolled her poetry with laudative zeal in his *A History of American Poetry* (1934), praising her success with the cinquains as "nothing less than extraordinary" and speaking of her other late poems as "perfect lyrics" ("Song," "Dirge," and "The Lonely Death") and "perfect Grecian quatrains" (unidentified).[15]

Edmund Wilson and Carl Sandburg also thought well of Crapsey's achievement,[16] as did Conrad Aiken to a lesser extent,[17] but it was Yvor Winters who was probably most responsible for keeping her name alive in a critical context. He regarded her as a "minor poet of great distinction," though without ignoring her flaws, which he saw as arising from a hypersensitivity that on occasion reached "the point of sentimentality."[18] A later essay went much further, referring to Crapsey as "certainly an immortal poet" and claiming that she had "been one of the most famous poets of our century."[19] The dubious nature of that last statement should not, however, obscure the genuine significance of his criticism as a whole, which firmly established—against the tide of popular disinterest—that Crapsey has always been "a lady obsessed with the necessity of writing well," one whose poetry was too valuable to lose.[20]

Unfortunately, in more recent times, critics and literary historians have lacked Winters's insight. In *A Short History of American Poetry* (1974), for example, Donald Barlow Stauffer relegates Crapsey to an inaccurate, patronizing aside amid an otherwise commendable discussion of Marianne Moore's debt to haiku: "One is reminded, too, of the *cinquains* of Adelaide Crapsey . . . who was also fascinated with the possibilities of syllabic verse."[21] Professor Hyatt H Waggoner's critical history, *American Poets: From the Puritans to the Present*, which appeared six years earlier, had not even mentioned Crapsey in passing.[22] This omission has been somewhat rectified by the first volume of Professor David Perkins's *A History of Modern Poetry* (1976), with the author briefly hailing Crapsey's "disciplined manipulation of form," her invention of the cinquain, again mistakenly presented as a syllabic formula, and her "severely impersonal" ability to project a sort of emotional impressionism.[23]

Recent anthologists have been equally remiss with regard to Crapsey's poetry. Not a single poem of hers appeared in Oscar Williams's *A Little Treasury of American Poetry*, the "revised" 1952 version, and Richard Ellmann's 1976 edition of *The New Oxford Book of American Verse* inexplicably suffers from the same lack, despite its much greater bulk.[24] Worse, in light of previous support, the last edition (1969) of Louis Untermeyer's *Modern American Poetry,* described as "New and Enlarged," also contains no Crapsey contribution.[25] Nor has the increasing popularity of literary feminism helped. Neither *Rising Tides: 20th Century American Women Poets* nor *Psyche: The Feminine Poetic Consciousness*, for instance, both printed in 1973, gives any indication that Adelaide Crapsey ever wrote poetry at all.[26] Even in Nancy Sullivan's anthology, *The Treasury of American Poetry* (1978), where an obvious, if ill executed, attempt is made to give female poets a greater say, Crapsey's name is among the missing.[27]

In general, it would seem that Crapsey has lost whatever audience she once had, and this during an era when the work of women artists in American culture is being brought to the attention of our society with increasing force. Perhaps the explanation for her continued neglect—excepting, of course, Professor Smith's definitive edition of her poems and letters—lies in the nature of her accomplishment, its dearth of confessional or rhetorical excesses, its dependence upon haiku-like compression for maximum effect. It is easy to understand, if not forgive, how a reader nurtured on the pyrotechnic virtuosities of, say, *Life Studies, Ariel,* or *Kaddish,* might find it difficult to relate to the diamond-small precision of "Amaze" and similar Crapsey works, where the intensity of the emotion being conveyed must evolve from a sudden, sharp, often subtle mating of idea and thing.

For a critic, the task remains to explain the dimensions and utlimate weight of Crapsey's achievement. In biographical terms, the only significant observation to be made is that Crapsey was not a "natural" poet by any means, in spite of her early love for the art. Though intelligent and well-educated, she had an interest in poetry which remained mainly scientific through most of her relatively short life, her own poetry providing little indication that she had the capacity for serious creative endeavors. It was only with the advent and advance of her illness that her modest talent was pointed in the right direction, given an obsession, and then pressured into a small Keatsian explosion after 1911.

Historically and aesthetically, it seems evident that Crapsey was at the forefront of the American branch of the movement towards Imagism, a pioneer in utilizing the example of Oriental techniques—which she apparently discovered on her own through the French versions—for clearing away the dense rhetoric common to traditional American and British verse at the turn of the century and helping to construct the platform from which Pound and Eliot would soon take flight. In fact, she anticipated Pound in many ways, and had already composed her series of memorable cinquains by the time he was writing in *The Fortnightly Review* about "Vorticism" and the compelling need for modern poets to assay—like the Japanese haiku masters—to capture "an intellectual and emotional complex in an instant of time."[28]

But this is not Crapsey's sole claim to attention, nor the only manner in which her poetry was distinctive and important. The way in which her best work reflected a cosmos without deity or possible salvation, its absence of a Christian perspective in direct opposition to her conventional reliance upon the Bible as a minister's daughter, certainly gave it a modern cast. She was also an innovator—though looking backwards to Dickinson for her prime models—in transforming American lyric poetry into a more individual vehicle of personal statement, "a poetry of personal identity" in the words of Gregory and Zaturenska.[29] As such, she deserves to be placed among "the cluster of women lyric poets" acclaimed by Louise Bogan, who "appeared on the American scene just before and after 1918" and "restored genuine and frank feeling to a literary situation which had become genteel, artificial, and dry."[30]

And yet, this aspect of Crapsey's *modus operandi* must not distort the opposing, equally valid view of Professor Perkins that Crapsey's poetry was "severely impersonal." Indeed, the paradox lies at the center of Crapsey's particular talent: her ability to adhere to the strict demands of strict forms, which she loved for themselves, while exploring the emotionally charged depths of a private anguish with brave candor. Thus, she prepared the ground for Imagism, at least in America, and opened the door to Millay and the later Teasdale at the same time, encompassing both through a skillful blending of extremes. In addition, her few longer, looser experiments at personal declarations of fierce despair and rebellion would seem to foreshadow, in a minor fashion, the path taken by Anne Sexton and Sylvia Plath decades later.

In a purely critical framework, however, the true test of Crapsey's worth still resides in the simple excellence of her strongest poetry. A significant group of cinquains—the successes and "near-misses" discussed in Chapter Five—and poems such as "Song," "The Lonely Death," and "To the Dead in the Grave-Yard Under My Window" affirm her genuine achievement as no amount of historical or analytical theorizing can. They alone proclaim her an authentic, if not a major, poet whose verses deserve to survive on their own merit.

Notes and References

Chapter One

1. The letters—many originals, some photostats—can be found among the Crapsey Papers at the University of Rochester Library, specifically in Box 1, Folders 1a through 6, and have been published in *The Complete Poems and Collected Letters of Adelaide Crapsey*, ed. Susan Sutton Smith (Albany, 1976), hereafter cited simply as *Poems and Letters*.

2. Edna St. Vincent Millay's first collection, *Renascence*, did not appear until 1917, although the controversy over the title poem and the *Century Magazine* verse contest had erupted five years earlier, while Millay was still in high school; see Jean Gould, *The Poet and Her Book: A Biography of Edna St. Vincent Millay* (New York, 1969), pp. 34-36, 38-40, and 55-56. Like Crapsey, Millay was a Vassar graduate (1917) and could very well have been influenced by Crapsey's *Verse* and perhaps moved by her tragically short life. Horace Gregory and Marya Zaturenska note a definite resemblance between the work of the two poets in their *A History of American Poetry* (New York, 1946), p. 94.

3. It seems reasonable to assume that Crapsey read Sara Teasdale's first two collections, *Sonnets to Duse and Other Poems* (New York, 1907) and *Love Songs* (New York, 1911). Both volumes certainly reflect the same vague commitment to an archaic, excessive, high Romantic style that hampered most of Crapsey's early poetry.

4. Mary Elizabeth Osborn, *Adelaide Crapsey* (Boston, 1933).

5. See Rev. Crapsey's autobiography, *The Last of the Heretics* (New York, 1924), pp. 124-26. Its title certainly suggests how willing, perhaps eager, Crapsey's father was to engage in public debate over his firm convictions.

6. Osborn, p. 8.

7. *Poems and Letters*, p. 6.

8. Crapsey, *The Last of the Heretics*, pp. 260, 266.

9. Ibid., p. vii.

10. See "Prison Methods" (Rochester, 1902) and "International Republicanism: The Way to Permanent Peace" (Philadelphia, 1918), two of his more famous sermons, as well as his controversial volumes on *Religion and Politics* (New York, 1905), *The Re-birth of Religion* (New York, 1907), *The Rise of the Working Class* (New York, 1914), and *The Ways of the Gods* (New York, 1921).

11. Accounts of his position on Christ as an historic rather than a mythic

110

figure and his subsequent heresy trial can be found in "Arguments for presentors and defense of Rev. A. S. Crapsey before the Court of Review of the Protestant Episcopal Church upon his appeal for judgment of the Court of the Diocese of Western New York" (New York, 1906) and "The Mangasarian-Crapsey debate" (Chicago, 1908).

12. Osborn, p. 14.

13. *Poems and Letters*, p. 3; Crapsey Papers, Box 1, Folder 1, scrapbook about Crapsey compiled by her mother.

14. Osborn, p. 22. Crapsey's penchant for male characters with last names only was perhaps an inherited British affectation, an easy literary means of humor, and perhaps also bespoke a certain lack of intimacy with members of the other sex.

15. Crapsey's address, entitled "The Open Road," was published in the *Kemper Hall Kodak* (June, 1897) and preserved by her mother in the scrapbook; Crapsey Papers, Box 1, Folder 1. In it, the author has taken obvious pains to organize her theme—man's "wandering spirit" through the ages and the need for her and her fellow graduates to continue that tradition in the name of science, humanity, and "pure adventure"—around appeals to a rich cultural and religious heritage, inserting references to Ulysses, Aeneas, Norse mythology, medieval Christianity (Knights of the Round Table), and the like.

16. In her article on Crapsey for the *Vassar Miscellany*, March 26, 1915, pp. 414-15, Jean Webster (McKinney) indicated that her friend's poetry was "almost . . . a by-product of her study in Metrics," and that she tossed off the early poetry as "the fleeting expression of a moment, and took no slightest care to preserve it."

17. *Poems and Letters*, pp. 8-9.

18. Adelaide Crapsey, *A Study in English Metrics* (New York, 1918), p. 7.

19. *Poems and Letters*, p. 10. The slips themselves are in the Crapsey Papers, Box 3, Folder 12.

20. A career and bibliographical guide from the Archives at Smith College, "Adelaide Crapsey, 1878-1914," states that "The Principles of Exposition" was a required course, dealing with "Themes affording practice in simple and natural expression on topics connected with the class work of the student."

21. In a brief memoir and review of *Verse* for the *New Republic*, January 31, 1923, p. 258, Louise Townsend Nicholl vividly recalled Crapsey's arrival at Smith: "a little new English teacher, on the campus, a small figure all in gray—gray shoes, gray dresses, gray capes, nothing but gray she wore—walking very softly but quickly."

22. *Poems and Letters*, p. 210.

23. Ibid., p. 216.

24. Ibid., pp. 222, 216.

25. Dr. Baldwin's memoir (dated March 19, 1923) is among the Crapsey Papers, Box 1, Folder 8.

26. Ibid., pp. 211-18 and 239-40.

27. Ibid., p. 251.

28. Ibid., pp. 229-33; also see Dr. Baldwin's memoir.

29. Ibid., p. 224.

30. Ibid., pp. 241-43.

31. Ibid., p. 244.

32. Ibid., p. 246.

33. Ibid., pp. 250-51.

34. Ibid., p. 252.

35. *Poets and Their Art* (New York, rev. 1967), p. 154.

36. *Forms of Discovery* (Chicago, 1967), p. 329.

37. Ironically, of course, George Santayana was a full-fledged member of that same tradition and accepted his role with typical, philosophic dispassion, as his preface to his own *Poems* (New York, 1922) makes clear: "Of impassioned tenderness or Dionysiac frenzy I have nothing. . . ."

38. Crapsey's annotated copy of *The Poems of John Keats* is in Box 3, Folder 13, of the Crapsey Papers; she had copied three of Landor's short poems, "Dirce," "On His Seventy-fifth Birthday," and the untitled "Mother, I cannot mind my wheel," into her Commonplace Book, which is in Box 2, Folder 3.

39. Crapsey Papers, Box 3, Folder 12. The slips indicate that she had consulted *The Poems of Charles Baudelaire* in a translation by F. P. Sturm, and Cyril Scott's translation of *The Flowers of Evil*, but that she had also read Baudelaire's *L'Art Romantique* in the original.

40. See Hideo Kawanami's essay, "Adelaide Crapsey and Michael Revon: Their Connection with Japanese Literature" (trans. Yoshiaki Arai) in the Crapsey Papers, Box 4, Folder 2.

41. Osborn, p. 109. Crapsey's biographer came upon a copy of Porter's book in the poet's Rochester library and naturally assumed that this was the source of the cinquain, since it offered both an Oriental connection and examples of five-line translations.

42. The copies are in Box 2, Folder 1, among holographs of Crapsey's own poems—Hideo Kawanami had been the one who found the translations first and realized what they were.

43. Actually, the Dickinson "discovery" had begun ten years earlier with the publication of *Poems by Emily Dickinson* (Boston, 1890), which was quickly followed by *Poems, Second Series* (Boston, 1891), *Letters of Emily Dickinson* (Boston, 1894), and then *Poems, Third Series* (Boston, 1896). But Stedman's anthology provided official recognition of Dickinson's importance—the Establishment had spoken.

44. Gregory, p. 97.

45. Osborn, p. 87.

46. While aware that Crapsey's decision to wear grey had sound economic and aesthetic reasons, I cannot agree with Professor Smith's belief that her

"dress seems to have been dictated by economy and by a sense of style and a personal flair quite different from the impulses prompting the white dresses of Emily Dickinson" ("The Poems of Adelaide Crapsey: A Critical Edition with an Introduction and Notes, "Doctoral dissertation, University of Rochester, 1972, p. lxxviii). The fact that Crapsey chose grey at Smith—a change from the brown outfits worn at Miss Lowe's—suggests a link with the greyness in her poetry, ever a symbol of bleak isolation and winter despair, and with Dickinson's proud but lonely role as a sensitive outsider, an eternal hermit, a chaste poet celebrating her tragic mask with witty deliberateness.

47. *Century* (November, 1914), 128. The magazine only printed the one poem, "The Witch," but Osborn claims (p. 104) that several had been accepted.

48. For a lucid and complete account of the textual variations in Crapsey's published works, see Smith, pp. xxix-xlv. Hereafter, the doctoral dissertation will always be identified by author's last name to distinguish it from *Poems and Letters*.

49. Some of the material used in her dissertation was altered or deleted when Professor Smith put together *Poems and Letters*; the sketch of the poet's life was changed for the better, but the discussion of textual variations in Crapsey's published work was unfortunately dropped.

50. *New Republic*, June 1, 1918, p. 153.

51. Baltimore *Post Express*, December 22, 1915; Crapsey Papers, Box 1, Folder 8.

Chapter Two

1. Class information is taken from a Vassar College memo issued to the school library by the College Recorder, dated November 19, 1959.

2. She must have read Browning in her "Nineteenth-Century Poetry" course, if not before.

3. Though virtually unread today, Lanier was a highly popular figure in late nineteenth-century American poetry, and it is easy to understand why young Crapsey might have been impressed by a poet so attached to Keatsian compounds, a Poe-like love of lush sound effects, and a deep Romantic commitment to a God-haunted world of unspoiled nature. His death from tuberculosis, the "poet's disease," would have also enhanced his attractiveness in Crapsey's eyes. See Sidney Lanier, *Centennial Edition of the Works*, ed. Charles R. Anderson (Baltimore, 1945) for Lanier's poetry and prose, and Edwin Mims, *Sidney Lanier* (Boston, 1905) for an interesting, if uncritical, account of his life.

4. Crapsey's poem appeared in the *Vassar Miscellany* (November, 1898), 71, and has since been reprinted in *Poems and Letters*, page number in text; hereafter, all page-number references to texts in Professor Smith's edition will be given in parentheses in the body of the text.

5. Poe was a legitimate Romantic, after all, especially in his poetry, which rhymed with a vengeance and maintained a distinctly early nineteenth-century taste for ambiguous metaphysical phenomena—echoes of Wordsworth and Byron, for instance, are never very difficult to find in his verses.

6. *Vassar Miscellany*, November, 1898, p. 94.

7. *Vassar Miscellany*, December, 1898, p. 137.

8. *Vassar Miscellany*, February, 1899, p. 229.

9. *Vassar Miscellany*, December, 1899, p. 148.

10. *Vassar Miscellany*, November, 1897, pp. 59-63.

11. *Vassar Miscellany*, May, 1898, pp. 396-99.

12. *Vassar Miscellany*, October, 1899, pp. 36-50.

13. The great influx of Irish immigrants, mostly poor and ill-educated, that had begun during the middle of the nineteenth century and continued until nearly the end of the century did indeed result in the rise of "boss politics," or at least an intensification of that problem, particularly in the Northeastern section of the country; it was frequently decried by both sincere Anglo-Saxon reformers and Nativist bigots.

14. *Vassar Miscellany*, January, 1900, pp. 223-29.

15. *Vassar Miscellany*, May, 1898, pp. 425-26.

16. "Eyes That See Not," *Vassar Miscellany*, December, 1898, pp. 128-29.

17. *Vassar Miscellany*, June, 1899, pp. 457-58.

18. *Vassar Miscellany*, November, 1899, pp. 128-29.

19. *Vassar Miscellany*, May, 1900, pp. 446-47.

20. *Vassar Miscellany*, December, 1900, pp. 133-35.

21. *Vassar Miscellany*, June, 1901, p. 470.

22. *Vassarion* (1899 Yearbook), pp. 118-26.

Chapter Three

1. Smith, p. lxxiv.

2. Crapsey Papers, Box 1, Folder 8.

3. Osborn, p. 109.

4. *Poems and Letters*, pp. 10-12. In an interview with Professor Smith, Esther Lowenthal recalled Crapsey working almost ceaselessly over her metrical study.

5. Esther Lowenthal, "An Introductory Note," in Adelaide Crapsey, *A Study of English Metrics* (New York, 1918), p. 6.

6. Smith, pp. lxviii-lxix.

7. *Poems and Letters*, pp. 194-96.

8. Crapsey Papers, Box 3, Folder 12.

9. Jean Webster, "Preface," in Adelaide Crapsey, *Verse* (New York, 1926), n.p.

10. Claude Bragdon, "Foreword," Ibid., n.p.

11. *A Study of English Metrics*, p. 7. Further references to this work are provided in parentheses in the text.

Chapter Four

1. "Preface," *Verse*, n.p.
2. See "Adelaide Crapsey's Poems," Louise Townsend Nicholl, *New Republic*, January 31, 1923, p. 258.
3. Undated letter in the Smith College Library Archives.
4. Letter dated October 11, 1914, Smith College Library Archives.
5. For the most lucid and accurate biography, see John Walsh, *Strange Harp, Strange Symphony: The Life of Francis Thompson* (New York, 1967), which corrects many of the pious distortions introduced by Wilfrid Meynell in his preface to the *Poems of Francis Thompson* (New York, 1913) and by Everard Meynell in *The Life of Francis Thompson* (London, 1913). The latter biography of the poet was the one Crapsey was reading in early January, 1914; see *Poems and Letters*, pp. 220, 225.
6. Crapsey Papers, Box 1, Folder 1 (Scrapbook).
7. Smith, p. lxi.
8. R. H. Super, *Walter Savage Landor* (New York, 1954).
9. Undated letter (c. 1960) to Mrs. Kirkett, in the Smith College Archives.
10. Landor's finest works were often prose, as in *Imaginary Conversations*, which occupy the most space in *Works* (London, 1853). The bulk of Landor's poetry was in Latin at a time when this practice had become eccentric, although he invariably turned to English when writing about his love life and other immediately autobiographical subjects.
11. *Poems and Letters*, p. 43.
12. Francis Thompson, an early student of Keats and Coleridge who leaned more toward Shelley later in life, would have to be considered here as well; see Walsh, pp. 15-16, 54, 88-91, 94-95, and 260-61.
13. *Poems and Letters*, pp. 188-99.
14. Pater, Hopkins, and Beardsley are but a few of the leading figures who sought to yoke their love of mystical extremes to the formalized, Baroque, presumably more ethical rituals of Roman Catholicism.
15. Stanley Weintraub, *Beardsley* (New York, 1967), p. 129. Like Beardsley, Oscar Wilde shared an interest in and taste for Oriental exotica, which was reflected in Whistler's work as well, and it is entirely possible that Crapsey's glances in the direction of the East were sparked by the fascination of the artists of the 1890s with that culture, just as their love of form, particularly French forms, undoubtedly influenced her.
16. Smith, p. 232.
17. Ibid., p. 114.
18. Louise Bogan, *A Poet's Alphabet*, ed. Robert Phelps and Ruth Limmer (New York, 1970), p. 427.

Chapter Five

1. Osborn, 109.

2. Crapsey never met any of her famous contemporaries in London, which is hardly surprising in view of her real poverty and daily isolation at the British Museum or some other local library.

3. Osborn, 109. Pound's work with Ernest Fenellosa's manuscripts had not commenced until after he had already met T. E. Hulme—Imagism's ostensible founder—and was working out his own Imagist (and later Vorticist) vein. For a thorough treatment of British and American involvement with Imagism, see J. B. Harner, *Victory in Limbo: A History of Imagism 1908-1917* (New York, 1975).

4. Michel Revon, *Anthologie de la Littérature Japonaise des Origines au XXe siècle* (Paris, 1910). Dr. Kawanami found three leaves of English and French poems among the Crapsey Papers which he recognized as copies of poems found in Revon's anthology and in Yone Noguchi's collection of original verses and translations from the Japanese, *From the Eastern Sea* (New York, 1910); see Smith, pp. lxxxvi-xc.

5. Noguchi's collection had originally appeared in London in 1903, seven years before its New York publication. Except for "Lines: from Basho" (p. 67), the rest of the brief lyrics in the book seem to be original compositions, though obviously steeped in Japanese poetic traditions. They betray, like Crapsey's own early work, a distinctly Georgian taste for hackneyed Romantic personifications and rhetorical excess, as in the typical "The Valley of Peace" (pp. 3-5): "Every bud hurried to greet the sunlight:/ The sunlight brought kisses/ For a fragrant place of Beauty and Life."

6. Osborn, p. 110.

7. *Poems and Letters*, pp. 24-25.

8. Noguchi, P. 67. The translation was, as usual, awkward and somewhat incomprehensible out of its Japanese context: "I have cast the world/ And think me as nothing,/ Yet I felt cold at snow-falling day,/ And happy on flower-day."

9. See Smith, pp. lxxxvi-xc.

10. Osborn, p. 89.

11. Ibid., p. 90.

12. *The Encyclopedia of Poetry and Poetics*, ed. Alex Preminger (Princeton, 1965), p. 126.

13. Despite the testimony cited by Osborn (pp. 89-90), this remains an essentially impressionistic conclusion, since Crapsey herself has left no description of the cinquain.

14. Crapsey's own arrangement for *Verse* has been reproduced in *Poems and Letters*, pp. 63-97.

15. Professor Smith, for instance, would probably want to include "Moon-shadows" and "Niagara" (*Poems and Letters*, pp. 38-39), while Yvor Winters would agree on "Niagara" and has included, among her "fine

poems," two other cinquains, "Snow" and "Roma Aeterna," although he hedges a bit with the observation that a "good many" of these "are slight, but all are distinguished, all are in their way honest and extremely perceptive"; see *Forms of Discovery* (Denver, 1967), pp. 330-31.

16. The opinion is shared by Yvor Winters; *Forms of Discovery*, p. 330.

17. Revon, p. 133.

18. Revon, p. 133, n. 2.

19. J. Isaacs, *The Background of Modern Poetry* (New York, 1952), p. 35.

20. Royall Snow, "Marriage with the East," *New Republic*, June 29, 1921, p. 139.

21. Smith, pp. xc-xci.

22. See *Poems and Letters*, p. 39; Winters, p. 330.

23. Professor Smith admires "Snow" for its "restrained and subtle variation on the theme of change and permanence," which seems to capture "the sensations of an entire season in a single sharp detail." That detail, however, does not add sufficient depth, in my estimation, to the poem to rescue it from superficiality; see *Poems and Letters*, p. 35.

24. Winters, p. 329.

25. Helen F. Birkett's letter (dated August 22, 1960) to an unnamed researcher alludes to the latter's theory about a "romantic disappointment" motivating some of the poems, including "The Guarded Wound," an idea which Miss Birkett found "very possible"; see Smith College Archives.

Chapter Six

1. *Shores of Light* (New York, 1952), p. 244.

2. Gregory, p. 94.

3. Osborn, p. 90. The friend was Elsie Draper.

4. Ibid., p. 90. It was the first two lines of "Lycidas" that seemed to intrigue Crapsey the most from the standpoint of vowel manipulations: "Yet once more, O ye laurels, and once more / Ye myrtles brown, with ivy never sere."

5. *Poems and Letters*, p. 233.

6. Osborn, p. 111.

7. Smith, p. cxviii. Gregory and Zaturenska are equally unimpressed: "The emotion she attempted to convey is clear enough, but as she wrote it down an unassimilated, all too Miltonic passion seemed to possess her lines, and that full expression of all she had to say seems thwarted of its final purpose and desires" (p. 96).

Chapter Seven

1. See the contemporary reviews collected in Mrs. Crapsey's scrapbook, Crapsey Papers, Box 1, Folder 1.

2. "Cinquains," *Others*, March, 1916, pp. 167-69.

Selected Bibliography

PRIMARY SOURCES

1. *Manuscripts*

NOTE: Detailed information about the Adelaide Crapsey papers at the University of Rochester Library can be found in John Rothwell Slater, "The Adelaide Crapsey Collection," *University of Rochester Library Bulletin* (Spring, 1961), pp. 37-40.

Claude Fayette Bragdon papers. University of Rochester Library. Rochester, New York.

Collection of Mr. and Mrs. Ralph Connor. LaGrangeville, New York.

Adelaide Crapsey papers. University of Rochester Library. Rochester, New York.

Adelaide Crapsey papers. Smith College Archives. Northampton, Massachusetts.

"Adelaide Crapsey, 1901" file. Alumnae Collection. Vassar College Library. Poughkeepsie, New York.

Algernon Sidney Crapsey papers. Rochester Public Library. Rochester, New York.

2. *Published Material*

A. Poetry Collections

SMITH, SUSAN SUTTON, ed. *The Collected Letters and Complete Poems of Adelaide Crapsey.* Albany: State University of New York Press, 1976. (Though copyrighted in 1976, this definitive text was not actually published until November, 1977.)

SMITH, SUSAN SUTTON, ed. "The Poems of Adelaide Crapsey: A Critical Edition with an Introduction and Notes." Doctoral dissertation, University of Rochester, 1972.

Verse. Foreword by Claude Bragdon. Rochester, New York: Manas Press, 1915.

Verse. Foreword by Claude Bragdon. Preface by Jean Webster. New York: Knopf, 1922; reprinted 1926, 1929, 1934, 1938.

B. Individual Poems

"Loneliness," *Vassar Miscellany,* November, 1898, p. 71.

"Time Flies," *Vassar Miscellany,* November, 1898, p. 94.

"The Heart of a Maid," *Vassar Miscellany,* December, 1898, p. 137.

"Repentance," *Vassar Miscellany,* February, 1899, p. 229.

120

"Hail Mary!" *Vassar Miscellany*, December, 1899, p. 148.
"The Witch," *Century*, November, 1914, p. 128.

C. Criticism
A Study in English Metrics. An Introductory Note by Esther Lowenthal.
New York: Knopf, 1918.

D. Short Stories (listed chronologically)
"A Girl to Love," *Vassar Miscellany*, November, 1897, pp. 59-63.
"The Knowledge He Gained," *Vassar Miscellany*, May, 1898, pp. 396-99.
"Mr. Percival Poynton and a Pig," *Vassar Miscellany*, October, 1899, pp.
36-50.
"Milord and Milady," *Vassar Miscellany*, January, 1900, pp. 223-29.

E. Book Reviews (listed chronologically)
[Review of *In Old Narragansett* by Alice Morse Earle], *Vassar Miscellany*,
May, 1898, pp. 425-26.
[Review of *Within the Hedge* by Martha Gilbert Dickinson], *Vassar Miscel-
lany*, June, 1899, 457-58.
[Review of *Stalky & Co.* by Rudyard Kipling], *Vassar Miscellany*,
November, 1899, pp. 128-29.
[Review of *Resurrection* by Leo Tolstoy], *Vassar Miscellany*, May, 1900, pp.
446-47.
[Review of *Richard Yea-and-Nay* by Maurice Hewlett], *Vassar Miscellany*,
December, 1900, pp. 133-35.

F. Stage Farce
"An Insane Episode," *Vassarion 99* Baltimore: Williamson and Wilkins,
1899, pp. 118-26.

G. Miscellaneous Prose
"Eyes That See Not," *Vassar Miscellany*, December, 1898, pp. 128-29.
"About College," *Vassar Miscellany*, June, 1901, p. 470.

SECONDARY SOURCES

1. *Biographical and Critical Studies*
BRAGDON, CLAUDE. *Merely Players*. New York: Knopf, 1929.
———*More Lives Than One*. New York: Knopf, 1938.
Despite their author's peculiar theories and "visions," these two memoirs
contain some interesting information about Crapsey and her life in
Rochester.
CRAPSEY, SIDNEY ALGERON. *The Last of the Heretics*. New York: Knopf,
1924. Extremely valuable intellectual autobiography that provides
many insights into the relationship between Crapsey and her liberal

father, though more through implication than direct references. The
emphasis throughout is on ideas rather than events, and the Rev.
Crapsey emerges as a curiously remote figure in terms of family life and
attitudes.

LOESCHER, WALTER C. "The Personality and Poetry of Adelaide Crapsey."
Master's thesis, University of Rochester, 1947. A solid, careful attempt
to define the mind behind the poetry and to relate the cinquain to
Japanese models and influences. The literary criticism is essentially
sound, particularly with regard to locating sources and defining Crapsey's poetic strengths. He views "To the Dead in the Grave-Yard Under
My Window" as "typical of the strongest and weakest sides of her poetic
development" and singles out the cinquains, "November Night,"
"Triad," "Shadow," "The Warning," "Niagara," and "Blue Hyacinths"
as representing "the high point" in Crapsey's "literary craftsmanship."

O'CONNOR, MARY EDWARDINE. "Adelaide Crapsey: A Biographical Study."
Master's thesis, University of Notre Dame, 1931. A pioneer study in
tracing Crapsey's poetry to her life, including the first description of the
cinquain as an accentual, not a syllabic, form. Contains much good
textual criticism.

OSBORN, MARY ELIZABETH. Adelaide Crapsey. Boston: Bruce Humphries,
1933. First and only biography of Crapsey to date, but criticism is
somewhat weak, except where obviously indebted to Sister O'Connor.
Sole source of the claim that Crapsey "actually developed the cinquain
late in the summer of 1909." Special value in its biographical details
resulting from interviews with the poet's mother and various friends,
colleagues, and teachers.

2. Selected Reviews, Essays and Parts of Books on Crapsey

ANDERSON, PEARL. "Miss Crapsey Reprinted," Poetry: A Magazine of Verse,
March, 1923. pp. 333-35. Essentially an uncritical review of the 1922
edition of Verse.

DEUTSCH, BABETTE. "Free Verse and Certain Strictures," Bookman,
January, 1920, pp. 496-98. Summarizes A Study of English Metrics
in an effort to relate it to contemporary work in prosody. More outline
than review.

FLETCHER, IAN. "Adelaide Crapsey's Cinquains," ADAM International
Review 35 (1970), 62-64. Insists upon comparison between Crapsey and
H. D., "that one true Imagist," and sees some similarities with early
Pound as well. Perceptive awareness throughout of the 1890s influence
at work in several of the cinquains, such as "Susanna and the Elders" and
"The Warning"—the latter is astutely linked to Walter De La Mare's
"Who?"

FLETCHER, JOHN GOULD. "The Orient and Contemporary Poetry," Asian
Legacy and American Life, ed. A. E. Christy. New York: John Day,
1945, pp. 145-72. Fletcher's essay alludes to Crapsey in passing but does

isolate the links between Imagism and the Orient, laying out the path from French lyrics to Japanese translations, although he seems unaware that Crapsey had anticipated the Imagists (himself included) in this respect.

FRASER, G. S. "Two Rochester Muses," *ADAM International Review* 35 (1970), 4-11. Though ostensibly devoted to Crapsey and Elizabeth Stanton Hardy, the attention is centered on Crapsey, whose metric study is deemed an "absolutely fresh contribution to metrical theory" and whose poetry is praised for its "Yankee" conciseness. Touches upon influence of haiku, tonka, and Imagism, along with a brief glance in the direction of preRaphaelite and Decadent echoes, and summarizes Crapsey's metrics.

GREGORY, HORACE AND MARYA ZATURENSKA. *A History of American Poetry*. New York: Harcourt, Brace, 1942, pp. 91-97. If a bit too enthusiastic at times, this remains the most intelligent critical description of Crapsey's achievement. Besides appreciating the enduring value of "Song" and understanding Crapsey's work in terms of projecting a "personal identity" and of a steady Miltonic influence, these two poet-critics were the first to detect the resemblance to Edna St. Vincent Millay.

HARTLEY, MARSDEN. *Adventures in the Arts*. New York: Boni & Liveright, 1921, pp. 207-14. A rather vague but occasionally insightful attempt to pin down Crapsey's unique virtues, which he labels "first rate poetic gifts" that encompass "sensibility of an exceptional order" and a "sense of economy." He notes the obvious connection between Crapsey and Emily Dickinson as well as H. D., and comprehends the pervasive debt owed to "Keats or Shelley."

HENDERSON, AICE CORBIN. "The Great Adventure," *Poetry: A Magazine of Verse*, September, 1917, pp 316-19. Reviews *Verse* in light of Crapsey's sad biography, stressing the need to keep the life and poetry separate, which she concedes she cannot do.

JONES, LLEWELLYN. *First Impressions*. New York: Knopf, 1925, pp 97-110. This essay by one of Crapsey's earliest and strongest supporters is really a combination of reviews previously published in various magazines. His criticism is solid for the most part, and it ranks Crapsey with Emily Dickinson and Alice Meynell as "one of the outstanding woman poets of the day," which reflects the condescending male attitude of the period. It includes a lucid commentary on *A Study in English Metrics* and evinces a perceptive awareness of the cinquain as an accentual formulation: "Miss Crapsey did not merely count syllables, but devised her five line poems in an iambic series."

KAWANAMI, HIDEO. "Adelaide Crapsey and Michel Revon: Their Connection with Japanese Literature," trans. Yoshioki Arai. *University of Osaka College of Commerce Anniversary Festschrift*, n.d. Located among the Crapsey papers at the University of Rochester Library (Box 4, Folder 2), this awkwardly translated (or perhaps awkwardly written) discussion of Crapsey's reading in and dependence upon Revon's translations in a pivotal study in any consideration of the precise, important debt Crapsey owed Japanese forms for her invention of the cinquain.

KREYMBORG, ALFRED. *A History of American Poetry: Our Singing Strength.* New York: Tudor, 1934, pp. 482-84. Crapsey is valued in the company of Lola Ridge, Mina Loy, and Marianne Moore for the originality of her accomplishment, and her cinquains are singled out for their control and artistry, each "a perfect rendition of a mood, each mood a contemplative view of life in the presence of death." Praises and quotes "Triad," "Release," "Fate Defied," "The Lonely Death," and four lines from "To the Dead in the Grave-Yard Under My Window," which is characterized as a "blank verse ode." Concludes that in "sheer perfection of artistry, no American has ever surpassed Adelaide Crapsey."

LEWIS, MARY DELIA. "Adelaide Crapsey," *Smith College Monthly,* December, 1915, pp. 113-16. A biographical review of *Verse* by a colleague of Crapsey's at Smith, more significant as memoir than as criticism, though ever conscious of the negative emotions at work behind the poet's best verses, including "Song."

MCKINNEY, JEAN WEBSTER. "Foreword Upon the Poems of Adelaide Crapsey," *Vassar Miscellany* 44 (1915), 414-15. Used as a Foreword to the Knopf editions of *Verse,* this brief comment by Crapsey's friend contains very little genuine criticism but does indicate Crapsey's preference for scholarship over creativity and her tendency to discard much of her early poetry "as the fleeting expression of a moment."

MONROE, HARRIET. *Poets and Their Art.* Revised Edition. New York: Books for Librarians, 1967, pp. 153-54. Originally written in 1932, this lush, impressionistic analysis by an early enthusiast for Crapsey's work occasionally hits a nerve, as when observing that the poet in confronting death "used her art like a sword to defend herself bitterly against the threatening enemy."

NICHOLL, LOUISE TOWNSEND. "Adelaide Crapsey's Poems," *New Republic,* January 31, 1923, p. 258. A brief review of the 1922 edition of *Verse* that takes Knopf to task for having meddled with the text Crapsey had "selected so exactingly and impersonally for the first edition." Besides emphasizing the cinquain as a stress pattern, this is also valuable for its biographical information—Nicholl was a freshman at Smith when Crapsey taught there and remembered her vividly.

PERKINS, DAVID. *A History of Modern Poetry.* Cambridge: Belknap, 1976, pp. 347, 364, 369, 371-72, 398. Though not familiar with the cinquain's accentual basis, Perkins does identify the "impersonal" element that seems to dominate Crapsey's strongest poetry. He neglects her longer efforts completely, however.

UNTERMEYER, LOUIS. *The New Era in American Poetry.* New York: Henry Holt, 1919, pp. 317-20. An oddly uneven though highly sympathetic attempt to place *Verse* within the context of its age, describing it gushingly as exhibiting "a sincerity of emotion and perfection of craft that proclaims the genius." Such exaggerations probably help explain the fundamental error in taste of equating "Triad" and "The Warning" with the much inferior "The Grand Canyon," although Untermeyer possesses enough of a saving instinct to appreciate the authentic worth of "Song" and "The Lonely Death."

WINTERS, YVOR. *In Defense of Reason.* Denver: Swallow, 1947, pp. 329-31. *Forms of Discovery.* Denver: Swallow, 1967, p. 568. Winters was one of the few sympathetic critics of Crapsey in the period between her death and the 1940s who tried to keep her name alive in the literary scene. His comments upon her debts to the writers of the 1890s and to French translations from the Japanese were generally valid and crucial, and his appreciation of Crapsey's poetry never clouded his perception of her weaknesses, her hypersensitivity, for example, to the "point of senti-mentality." Only later, in *In Defense of Reason,* perhaps under pressure of the continued neglect of Crapsey, did he become somewhat silly in his championing of her work, designating her "an immortal poet" and speaking of her as "one of the most famous poets of our century."

Index

(The works of Crapsey are listed under her name)

126